LUDWIG VAN BEETHOVEN

Fidelio

OPERA STUDY GUIDE

WITH

LIBRETTO

OPERA CLASSICS LIBRARY™SERIES

Edited by Burton D. Fisher
Principal lecturer, *Opera Journeys Lecture Series*

Opera Journeys™ Publishing / Boca Raton, Florida

Copyright © 2018 by Opera Journeys Publishing

All rights reserved

No part of this publication may be reproduced, stored in a retrieval system, or transmitted, in any form or by any means, electronic, mechanical, photocopying, recording, or otherwise, without the prior permission from Opera Journeys Publishing.

All musical notations contained herein are original transcriptions by Opera Journeys Publishing.

WEB SITE: www.operajourneys.com   E MAIL: operaj@bellsouth.net

Contents

Opera Journeys™ *Mini Guide Series*

Opera Classics Library™ *Series*

Opera Journeys™ *Libretto Series*

A History of Opera:
Milestones and Metamorphoses

Mozart's Da Ponte Operas

PUCCINI COMPANION

Verdi Companion: 27 Opera Study Guide

<u>*Over 125 GUIDES & LIBRETTI AVAILABLE: Print or Ebook*</u>

•The Abduction from the Seraglio •Adriana Lecouvreur •L'Africaine •Aida
•Andrea Chénier •Anna Bolena •Ariadne auf Naxos •Armida •Attila
•The Ballad of Baby Doe •The Barber of Seville •Duke Bluebeard's Castle
•La Bohème •Boris Godunov •Candide •Capriccio •Carmen
•Cavalleria Rusticana •Cendrillon •La Cenerentola •La Clemenza di Tito
•Le Comte Ory •Così fan tutte •The Crucible •La Damnation de Faust
•The Death of Klinghoffer •Doctor Atomic •Don Carlo •Don Giovanni
•Don Pasquale •La Donna del Lago •The Elixir of Love •Elektra •Ernani
•Eugene Onegin •Exploring Wagner's Ring •Falstaff •La Fanciulla del West
•Faust •La Fille du Régiment •Fidelio •Die Fledermaus •The Flying Dutchman
•Die Frau ohne Schatten •Der Freischütz •Gianni Schicchi •La Gioconda
•Hamlet •Hansel and Gretel •Henry VIII •Iolanta •L'Italiana in Algeri
•Les Huguenots •Iphigénie en Tauride •Julius Caesar •Lakmé •Lohengrin
•Lucia di Lammermoor •Macbeth •Madama Butterfly •The Magic Flute
•The Makropolis Case •Manon •Manon Lescaut •Maria Stuarda
•The Marriage of Figaro •A Masked Ball •Die Meistersinger •The Mikado
•Nabucco •Nixon in China •Norma •Of Mice and Men •Orfeo ed Euridice
•Otello •I Pagliacci •Parsifal •The Pearl Fishers •Pelléas et Mélisande
•Porgy and Bess •Prince Igor •I Puritani •The Queen of Spades
•The Rake's Progress •The Rape of Lucretia •The Rhinegold •Rigoletto
•The Ring of the Nibelung •Roberto Devereaux •Rodalinda •Roméo et Juliette
•La Rondine •Der Rosenkavalier •Rusalka •Salome •Samson and Delilah
•Show Boat •Siegfried •Simon Boccanegra •La Sonnambula •Suor Angelica
•Susannah •Il Tabarro •The Tales of Hoffmann •Tannhäuser •Thaïs •Tosca
•La Traviata •Tristan and Isolde •Il Trittico •Les Troyens •Il Trovatore
•Turandot •The Valkyrie •Werther •West Side Story •Wozzeck

WWW.OPERAJOURNEYS.COM

a *Prelude*........

OPERA CLASSICS LIBRARY's
Fidelio
STUDY GUIDE WITH LIBRETTO

In 1954, after the death of Stalin in Soviet Russia, performances of *Fidelio* became a statement of outrage for those who were unjustly condemned to the regime's prisons. And when Vienna was liberated from the Soviet yolk in 1955, the reopened Staatsoper performed *Fidelio*, beaming it to listeners over loudspeakers — at times some became so emotionally overcome that they envisioned miracles being performed.

But *Fidelio* is also a testament to married love. In 1941, Kirsten Flagstad left America to join her husband in Norway, who had been a collaborator with the Nazis. But after the war she defended her actions by performing *Fidelio* as a testament to her love and heroism, as she remained at her husband's side while the surrounding world embraced insanity.

Ernest Newman commented on the universal ideals that saturate Beethoven's works: "Again and again (Beethoven) lifts us to a height from which we re-evaluate not only his music, but all life, all emotion, and all thought."

Beethoven believed in noble ideals: equality, the brotherhood of humanity, the loving interdependence of man and woman, and the just providence of God. But above all, Beethoven believed in the resilience of the human spirit in the face of oppression and tyranny. Those ideas remain at the core of *Fidelio*, Beethoven's sole opera.

The opera endures because it represents a liberating experience; a story that ennobles the cornerstones of human aspirations — universal brotherhood, love, and compassion. *OPERA CLASSICS LIBRARY* explores Beethoven's *Fidelio* with a *Commentary and Analysis* that deals with the opera's genesis, biographical and chronological elements, and its premiere and performance history.

The text also contains a *Brief Story Synopsis, Principal Characters,* and a *Story Narrative with Music Highlight Examples,* the latter containing original music transcriptions that are interspersed within the story's dramatic exposition. In addition, the text includes a *Dictionary of Opera and Musical Terms.*

The *Libretto* provides an English translation, side-by-side.

The opera art form is the sum of many artistic expressions: theatrical drama, music, scenery, poetry, dance, acting and gesture. In opera, the music composer who is the dramatist; he applies the emotive power of his music and the kinetic intensity of the prose to provide powerful theater, an impact on one's sensibilities that can reach into the very depths of the human soul.

Burton D. Fisher
Editor
OPERA CLASSICS LIBRARY

Fidelio

"Leonore, oder Der Triumph der ehelichen Liebe"
("Leonore, or The Triumph of Married Love")

An opera (singspiel) in German in two acts

Music
by
Ludwig van Beethoven

Libretto: Joseph Sonnleithner,
with successive revisions by
Stephan van Breuning and Friedrich Treitschke

Premiere: Vienna, 1805

Commentary and Analysis

L udwig van Beethoven (1770 — 1827) was a child prodigy; his genius was conspicuous as a skilled pianist, violinist and organist. A cornerstone of his talent was his incredible memory; at a young age he memorized all the Preludes and Fugues from Bach's Well-Tempered Clavichord. Beethoven's father, a failed tenor, intended to exploit his son's talents in the same manner as Leopold Mozart exploited young Wolfgang: it is reported that he beat the young Beethoven to practice, and forbid him to improvise, an unjust strictness that surely planted the seeds of Beethoven's later revolt against every kind of authority.

The young Beethoven grew up in poverty and suffering: he witnessed the death of three of his siblings and his father destroying himself with alcohol abuse, his mother dying of consumption at a young age. At 18, the young Beethoven was forced to assume full responsibility of what was left of his destitute family.

Beethoven left his native Bonn for Vienna, a city that was thriving in music and the arts. His talents thoroughly impressed Mozart, who commented, "Watch this young man. One day he will give the world something to talk about." In 1789, he was commissioned to compose the Cantata on the Death of Joseph II, a work of unusual intensity and dramatic power from a very young composer. But it was Beethoven's incredible talent at improvisation that mesmerized the patronizing nobility; they sponsored "improvisational contests" that pitted pianist against pianist, with each competing to embellish the improvisations of the other. In the end, Beethoven was always the victor.

In 1791, at 21, Beethoven had established his fame as a pianist, the first of the late eighteenth-century piano virtuosos; he possessed a charismatic style that was uncharacteristically unique for its time. Before Beethoven, Mozart and Hummel had established smooth and fluent playing styles, but Beethoven's goal was to inject into keyboard expression a hitherto unexploited sense of orchestral power and sonority; his hands would hover high above the keyboard before crashing down in a powerful attack that at times would break strings. Pianists before Beethoven suavely and elegantly wooed their audiences, but Beethoven's goal was to deliver explosive keyboard pyrotechnics.

Nevertheless, Beethoven had a consuming passion to compose music; from the very beginning his musical talents were those of a creator rather than a performer. Contextually, Beethoven was a force of nature that could not be contained, a musician who was extremely confident in his own genius, natural talents, ideas, and originality. He looked upon the existing rules of harmony with suspicion, which made it impossible for him to teach. One teacher commented, "He has not learned anything and he never will. He is hopeless." But Beethoven heard music differently than his contemporaries; he wrestled with harmony and playing technique so that his music spoke a new and unprecedented emotional language. Powerful thoughts and ideas about humanity were stirring within his musical soul, and he was determined to use the musical language to express enlightened, noble ideals.

B etween 1796 and 1798, Beethoven contracted meningitis; his hearing became impaired, which signalled the beginning of his epic and heroic battle against deafness. By 1817, he was totally deaf, and in his despair he complained that he was unable to hear the sublime sounds of his own music. Nevertheless, he functioned in torment and agony, guided by the passion of the music that was throbbing within his soul.

Beethoven's early compositions mirrored his predecessors, such as the eighteenth-century Classicism of Mozart and Haydn. But in 1805, Beethoven reinvented the expressive foundation of his compositional style with the Symphony No. 3, the "Eroica"; the symphony was originally dedicated to Napoleon at a time when he appeared to be a champion of the enlightenment principles of human rights and freedom, but after Napoleon crowned himself Emperor, Beethoven sensed elements of ambition and a lust for power; the enraged composer remove the dedication of the symphony to that of an unnamed hero — quite simply, a hero of the spirit and symbol of man's noblest aspiration. But in the end it may have been Beethoven who was the hero striding through the massive framework of the Eroica, furiously waging a battle against deafness, but refusing to surrender to it.

As musical expression entered the nineteenth century, the Eroica became a monumental turning point in musical history — it represented music in a new style, scope and dimension. The Symphony represented Beethoven's true voice: serious humanistic ideas were expressed with a pyrotechnic display of mastery, a new style of virtuosity, a massive sonority, profound Romantic expression, rhythmic richness, an unconventionality of form, and complex harmonies and dissonances of fierce and titanic force. His music was so emotionally profound, inspiring, and surging with energy that its listener's became captivated, in a sense, virtually paralyzed by its intensity.

Beethoven's personal life was chaotic. He gave piano lessons to many women of noble birth who he was subconsciously drawn to, but they were unattainable because of their social status — the "van" of Beethoven's name represented his affectation, and was not a sign of property or breeding. In the end, Beethoven was rejected by the social world and expressed the rejection of his social status in emotional rages that made him seem insane. Nevertheless, Beethoven's battle with deafness served to feed his despair.

A succession of masterpieces continued during the early years of the nineteenth century: the first version of *Fidelio* (1805); three Razumovsky Quartets; the Violin Concerto, Piano Concertos Nos. 4 in G, and 5 in E-flat; Symphonies Nos. 4 through 8; and several of the composer's famous sonatas — the Waldstein and Appassionata, among the many.

Beethoven's last years were consumed by spiritual conflict and despair. A tragic muse was guiding the pen of a deaf composer, which forced Beethoven to retire into his inner world from which he composed gigantic and mysterious works: Missa Solemnis; the final String Quartets of Opus 130; and many of the piano sonatas.

Beethoven began his composition career expressing the Classical tradition of elegance and dignity, but ended that career as a composer of works possessing profound cosmic and human significance — he was a complex and intense man who bared his soul through his music, which he concluded was being composed for eternity.

Beethoven possessed decidedly revolutionary notions about the internal structure of human society. He wouldl express those conficts and tensions to his pupil, Carl Czerny: "What is in my heart must come out so I write it down." Like Richard Wagner, Beethoven had difficulty adapting to the existing mores of society — and he had concluded that the world must adapt to him. So he extended musical structures by inventing his own musical language — the expressions were cryptic, explosive, and propulsive, with rhythmic music and with accentuations (sforzandos) that at times seemed to overturn existing metrical patterns.

To the Romantics, Beethoven's music possessed transcendental qualities: it was revelatory music that united humanity; it was a manifestation of the Divine that possessed the power to transform, fill and shape silence, change moods and express ideas that transcended words.

The Ninth Symphony (1824) captured the imagination of the Romantics: musically it defied existing forms, and represented a spiritual experience and call for brotherhood through its titanic explosion of musical ideas. It was the Beethoven work that most influenced Berlioz and Wagner, and ultimately remained the unachievable ideal of Brahms, Bruckner and Mahler.

In 1926, Beethoven's funeral was a public tribute reportedly attended by some 20,000 people. The world and human lives had changed through Beethoven's music — the composer had shared his soul in a sublime expression of the musical language that possessed extraordinary grandeur and spirit.

Beethoven's legacy represents a powerful body of music that endures because it mirrors humanity: it is saturated with storm and conflict; Beethoven was using the musical language to remind humanity of the precious nature of human life — a worthy aspiration that must be ennobled through love, hope and compassion.

A t the turn of the eighteenth century, Germans were preoccupied with the state of their musical theater; in particular, they were dismayed with the failure of opera to express and identify with their cultural identity. The thrust of new developments in the lyric theater materialized with the German Romanticist movement, beginning wth Carl Maria von Weber's *Der Freischütz* (1821).

The Singspiel Theatre opened in Vienna (1778), but few other national operas of any substance followed: Vienna remained saturated with French and Italian imports, in particular, Cherubini's spectacle lyric theater works. As such, the composition of a new German opera became an event of profound interest, culturally and musically. The Viennese music world looked to Beethoven — and Emmanuel Schikaneder (1748 — 1812), a theatrical jack-of-all trades, as its resuer. In March 1803, it was reported that Beethoven was composing an writing an opera for the Theater an der Wien; in August of that same year, the text of the new opera was undertaken by Schikaneder.

Schikaneder was distinguished throughout Europe as an actor, singer and writer. In 1791, he had become the spiritual force guiding Mozart's composition of *Die Zauberföte* ('The Magic Flute') for his suburban Viennese playhouse — the libretto was written by Schikaneder and Carl Ludwig Giesecke.

Schikaneder's theatrical legacy remains controversial: he has been variously regarded as an errant rogue as well as a wayward genius — a consummate showman with solid theatrical instincts. After emerging from a childhood of immense poverty, he became an itinerant fiddler, and then an entrepreneurial theater manager. He eventually graduated to acting and toured in his own company, variously portraying the title roles in *King Lear, Macbeth*, and *Hamlet*.

In both life and art, Beethoven was a severe moralist. He often complained that Mozart had squandered his talent in composing music to such ridiculous libretti as *Don Giovanni* and *Così fan tutte;* however, he did approve of *Die Zauberföte*, which he not only considered a true German singspiel, but he raved about the soul of its underlying theme —light triumphant over darkness, and good over evil, represented universal humanistic ideals.

Nevertheless, any relationship between Schikaneder and Beethoven was seemingly antithetic: Schikaneder thrived as a pure showman, which he demonstrated by his clownish portrayal of clown Papageno in *Die Zauberföte*. In contrast, Beethoven's soul was immersed in noble human aspirations. Beethoven yearned to compose an opera and was seeking a subject that would inspire his talents. Schikaneder's choice for an opera failed to inspire Beethoven: *Vestas Feuer*, with a plot set in ancient Rome, the project abandoned after the completion of only two scenes.

The eighteenth-century Enlightenment awakened the soul of Europe to renewed optimism: a hope that democratic progress would consolidate egalitarian ideals, and that the economic growth and industrialization of Europe would decrease the disparity between wealth and poverty. The Enlightenment inspired the French Revolution, which began with the storming of the Bastille in 1789.

Enlightenment ideals embraced a new world order incorporating humanistic ideals of freedom and civility. But those ideals ultimately became a mirage and illusion as the original elevated hopes and dreams dissolved in the devastation of the Reign of Terror (1892 — 1894). In addition, a universal sense of despair was reinforced by Napoleon's preposterous despotism, the post-Napoleonic return to autocratic tyranny and oppression, and the economic and social injustices nurtured by the Industrial Revolution.

Like the Holocaust of the twentieth century, those bloodbaths shook the very foundations of humanity by invoking man's deliberate betrayal of his highest nature and ideals: Schiller was prompted to reverse the idealism of his exultant "Ode to Joy" (1785), and ultimately concluded that the new century had "begun with murder's cry." To the Romanticists — the pessimists of the nineteenth century — the drama of human history was approaching doomsday, and civilization was on the verge of completely vanishing. Others concluded that the French Revolution and the Reign of Terror had ushered in a terrible new era of unselfish crimes in which men committed horrible atrocities out of love not of evil but of virtue. Like Goethe's *Faust*, who represented "two souls in one breast," man was considered a paradox, simultaneously the possessor of great virtue and wretched evil.

The horror of the French Revolution's Reign of Terror inspired many dramas that addressed the perils, sufferings, and heroism of that feverish epoch. As such, Post-Revolutionary France witnessed a flowering of highly dramatic stage works with patriotic and political themes, such as unjust imprisonment, escape and rescue. In dramas of the latter, the hero or heroine would be imprisoned by a villainous tyrant, and a spouse would attempt to free the other, invariably resulting in a happy ending and the arrest of tyrant.

In 1803, Schikaneder was manager of the Theater an der Wien and asked Beethoven to write an opera for his theater; he strongly approved of the composer's choice of *Fidelio*, a story whose underlying theme dealt with freedom from human suffering caused by injustice, as well as the transcendence of married love. Beethoven treasured the human ideals of the story, a testament to the hopes of every victim of oppression and tyranny, that highlighted man's aspirations for love — the latter extremely personal to a man such as Beethoven who never married.

The genesis of the underlyng *Fidelio* story is attributed to a popular autobiographical story by Jean-Nicolas Bouilly, and presumably represented a factual account of his experiences and those of his family after being trapped in the furor of the Reign of Terror: *Léonore, ou L'amour conjugal* ("Leonore, and Married Love"). In 1798, the composer Pierre Gaveaux (1761 — 1825) transformed the story into an opera that was produced at the Feydeau Theatre in Paris. In 1804, Ferdinando Paër, then Kapellmeister at Dresden; produced *Eleonora, ossia l'Amore conjugale,* the Italian opera version of the same Bouilly story; and in 1805, Simon Mayr, a Bavarian choirmaster at Bergamo, composed an opera based on the identical story.

In 1803, Beethoven became composer-in-residence at Schikaneder's Theater an der Wien. His moral convictions and sympathy for the Bouilly story were so profound that he could not be undeterred from composing an opera dealing with the same subject. The story represented a vivid and serious drama about real contemporary people, however, Beethoven's underlying inspiration evolved from its overwhelming moral message: that adversity can be conquered by loyalty, love, and heroic resolve.

In 1804, Baron Peter von Braun bought the Theater an der Wein from Schikaneder; it reepresented the beginning of a stormy relationship between Beethoven and the impresario. Joseph von Sonnleithner (1765 —1835), the secretary of the imperial theaters, was entrusted with writing the German version of Bouilly's book for the forthcoming *Fidelio.* Applying unabated energy, Beethoven completed *Fidelio* in the summer of 1805. Rehearsals began immediately. Nevertheless, *Fidelio* heralded the beginning of almost a decade of anguish and sorrow for Beethoven and his treasured opera.

Beethoven had composed the opera's music in a style that demanded virtually superhuman capabilities from singers; in the end, its difficulty prompted the singers to condemn the work as unsingable. They begged Beethoven to make modifications in the score, but he adamantly refused. During orchestra rehearsals, Beethoven agonized; he was unable to cope with the orchestra's sloppy musicianship, and in particular, their failure to heed to his musical dynamics — those *sforzandos,* or sudden bursts of volume that were even stronger than accents.

In November 1805, *Fidelio* premiered at Vienna's Theater an der Wien. A week earlier, French troops had occupied Vienna with Napoleon esconcing himself at the Schönbrunn Palace — the Austrian Emperor, the aristocracy and nobility, and most of the wealthy Viennese patrons had already deserted the capital.

Fidelio was a devastating failure: its three acts made the opera too long, and its theme of the triumph of freedom over oppression was distasteful and anathema to an audience largely comprised of French troops. Additionally, the opera had been inadequately rehearsed, and the singers, for the most part, were unequal to their tasks: the Leonore (Anna Milder), later to establish a distinguished career under her married name of Milder-Hauptmann, was too young and inexperienced; the Florestan (Friedrich Christian Demmer) was a singer of limited vocal and intellectual capacity. The overture played at the production of this First Version of *Fidelio,* known today as Leonora No. 2. The opera was canceled after two performances.

According to biographer J. A. Röckel, after the premiere disaster, there was a meeting of some of Beethoven's sincerest well-wishers in the home of Prince Lichnowsky. All were distressed by *Fidelio's* failure and unwilling to recognize or accept any inherent flaws in the work — nevertheless, they were determined to consider ways and means of resurrecting the opera.

Their stormy session lasted into the early morning: number-by-number was played on the piano, sung, and discussed in critical detail. Initially, Beethoven vehemently opposed nearly every suggestion made to remedy the defects of the libretto and score.

But he ultimately yielded to his own obstinacy and was persuaded to provide a drastic surgical modification of *Fidelio*. For purposes of condensation, he consented to sacrifice some of the music and remodel the libretto: three numbers were excised in their entirety, and the action was reduced from three to two acts. Most importantly, the rearrangement of the libretto was placed in the astute hands of Stephan von Breuning, a proven theatrical master.

The newly revised *Fidelio* was staged in March 1806, four months after its original premiere: Röckel sung the role of Florestan, replacing Demmer; the overture played on that occasion is known today as the Leonora No. 3. This Second version of *Fidelio* seemed headed for success, but Beethoven encountered vociferour quarrels with Baron von Braun, the theaster manager after accusing him of withholding receipts. As a result, Beethoven withdrew *Fidelio* from the Theater an der Wein — the last that would be heard of *Fidelio* for several years.

In 1814, members of the Court Theatre company were seeking a vehicle for a benefit performance. By this time, Beethoven's popularity in Vienna was unrivaled, and a revival of Beethoven's idealistic *Fidelio* seemed appropriate considering current political events. It would appear to be ironical, since it coincided with meetings of the Congress of Vienna, which was deciding the fate of Napoleon and France. Beethoven agreed to resurrect his opera, but with the condition that the revision of the text and action be entrusted to Georg Friedrich Treitschke (1776 —1842), the renowned poet and stage manager at the Kärnthnerthor Theatre.

Treitschke had achieved distinguished stage accolades, and was determined to inject many dramatic changes that would serve to modernize the wording of the libretto. Treitschke later recalled that the greatest challenge was the opening scene of the second act, in which Florestan first appears in the dark dungeon. Beethoven wanted the suffering Florestan to have an aria in which he could distinguish himself, but Treitschke believed that credibility would be severely tested if a man at the point of death by starvation would be pouring out his sould by singing. The compromise became Treitschke's additional text that expressed the last flames of life before they are about to extinguish. Thus, following Florestan's opening statement, "Gott! Welch Dunkel hier!" ("God! What darkness here!"), the debilitated prisoner imagines Leonore, his consoling angel, rescuing him from his dungeon to freedom: "Ein Engel, Leonoren, Leonoren, der Gattin so gleich, der, der führt mich zue Freiheir in's himmlische Reich." ("An angel, Leonore, Leonore, my adored wife. She leads me to freedom, where there is no more pain." In another Treitschke revision, the final act was divided into two scenes in order to emphasize the symbolic transformation from darkness to daylight.

For nine years, *Fidelio* had been Beethoven's child of sorrow, but it was an opera whose underlying ideas were firmly implanted in the composer's soul. In the end, Treitschke's literary talents served to become the metaphorical "rescuer" of Beethoven's cherished *Fidelio*. The composer was delighted with Treitschke's revisions, which he expressed in his later compliments: "They are determined that I rebuild the desolate ruins of an old castle."

Beethoven made changes in the music of almost every part of the original opera. The re-writing proceeded slowly. At one point, he claimed, "The first act will be finished in a few days, but there is still much to be done in the second, as well as a fresh overture to be written, which, however, will be the easiest part of all, because I can compose an entirely new one." Nevertheless, by the time of the first performance of the new *Fidelio*, the new overture was not ready.

In May 1814, the Third Version of *Fidelio* was performed at the Kärnthnerthor Theater in Vienna; *Fidelio* finally enjoyed its first emphatic success. Among the additions to the music score it included Rocco's now well-known aria in praise of money, "Hat man nicht auch Gold beineben" ("If you have no gold, then happiness is not secure"), although that aria appeared in the First Version of 1805, but was deleted from the Second Version.

Fidelio was given in Prague in November 1814, with the original Leonore No. 2 overture, which Beethoven had earlier discarded because he considered it too light for the drama. The performance began with Beethoven's *The Ruins of Athens Overture*: the new overture, the E major, that is now known as the *Overture to Fidelio*, was first heard at the second performance, two days later.

From the opera's infancy, Beethoven had desired that his opera be entitled *Leonore*, but in 1805 the theater authorities insisted on *Fidelio*, no doubt out of regard for Paër and Mayr's "Leonore" operas that dealt with the same subject. For the 1814 revival, Beethoven again fought for the title "Leonore," and the original libretto for those performances cited the title as "Leonore." However, in a copy preserved in the Vienna Opera archives, "Leonore" has been struck out in red crayon — and *Fidelio* was substituted. It seems that once more Beethoven had been unable to succeed against the conflicts and tensions of theater management, and for posterity, his sole opera remains his beloved *Fidelio*.

The greatness of a work of art may perhaps be the coefficient of the degrees of criticism it receives. Since the inception, *Fidelio* has been the recipient of much positive as well as negative criticism. Some critics have condemned the opera as eclectic: that it seems to pulsate from singspiel, to music drama, to melodrama, to oratorio. Some detractors consider the libretto a contrived and improbable scenario, although Bouilly was been unequivocal in vowing that it represents a true account of his own experiences during the Reign of Terror.

And to some, the subplot involving the love triangle of Marzelline, Jaquino and Fidelio is trivial and inferior, if not an embarrassment to the dramatic intensity of the ensuing drama. In effect, the heroine, Leonore/Fidelio, is involved in two plots: the entanglement in the love triangle with Marzelline and Jaquino; and her heroic adventure to rescue Florestan that ultimately resolves in the deadly confrontation with Pizarro.

Beethoven's musical characterizations are almost Mozartian in their hierarchy. As soon as Fidelio (Leonore) enters the scene the entire score begins a transformation — from the light texture of the Marzelline-Jaquino dispute to a mood of darkness and gravity. The music distinguishes the characters: all of the music for Leonore and Florestan is dramatic and somber, but characteristically light for Rocco, Marzelline and Jaquino, and dark and sinister for the evil Pizarro.

The plot is deeply immersed in an immensely powerful spirit of noble human ideals: a tension between sacrifice, marital fidelity, courage, hope, and freedom from political oppression and injustice. The words describing those ideals resound in the libretto and become the opera's soul: "Freiheit" (freedom), "Pflicht" (duty), and "Leben" (life).

But it is character of the heroine Leonore who fired Beethoven's imagination and inspired his muse. In Goethe's *Faust*, woman was ennobled: "Das Ewig-Weibliche Zieht uns hinan." ("The eternal woman draws us onward."); Goethe and the German

Romanticists ennobled the woman who could redeem man's egotism and narcissism through her unbounded love, understanding, wisdom, and sacrifice. Leonore represents that quintessential "ewige-weibliche" or Goethe's "eternal female" — the female ideal that frees a man from the prison of himself. Leonore, the ideal of conjugal love, was the woman Beethoven sought in vain all of his life, but without success.

Beethoven endowed Leonore with intensely dramatic moments in which to express her love and courage. In her great Act I aria, beginning with the recitative, "Abscheulicher! Wo eilst du hin?" ("You vile monster! What will you do?"), she responds to overhearing Pizarro's nefarious plans to destroy his prisoner, and her emotions explode as she calls for love and hope to end her suffering: "Komm, Hoffnung lass den letzten Stern." ("Come, let a star of hope not be denied me.")

In Act II, she observes the prisoner as she and Rocco dig the grave and she proclaims with profound compassion that whoever the prisoner is, he shall not perish, and she will free him from his chains. And in that courageous, heroic moment, she protects Florestan from Pizarro: "Tödt'erst sein Weib!" ("First kill his wife!") And at the moment of when Florestan's rescue is evident the text conveys the essence of Goethe's "ewige-weibliche": Florestan inquires of Leonore, "What have you done for me? And she replies, "Nothing, nothing, my Florestan."

Beethoven specifically designed the Act I Quartet in the canon form: "Mir ist so wunderbar" ("How marvelous it is") is in a contrapuntal style of two or more voice parts in which the melody is imitated exactly and completely by each successive voice, though not always at the same pitch. In Verdi's Quartet from *Rigoletto*, each of the characters is delineated by different music, but Beethoven was not composing four separate melodies to emphasize the character's words: in the *Fidelio* canon, each character sings the same melody, perhaps a subtle suggestion that each shares a common responsibility for human goodness and virtue. Nevertheless, each character is caught up with different emotions: Leonore is consumed by hope and resolve; Rocco is in conflict with materialism, and Marzelline and Jaquino indulge in childishness associated with love.

In the finale of Act I the oppressed prisoners are released from their cells and immediately indulge in a joyous celebration of that longed-for moment of daylight and air: "O welche Lust! In frier Luft den Athem leicht zu heben" ("Oh what joy! To be released from gloom and be revived by the air.") It is a moment of intense pathos as a young prisoner admonishes another to fortify his faith and hope: "Let us put out trust in God's help. I still hear Hope saying softly to me. We will be free, we will find peace, and we will find peace." Those words echo the underlying theme of *Fidelio*: that there is always hope that humanity can be rescued from tyranny and oppression.

Pizarro is a one-dimensional character: a villainous and sinister man of consummate evil, constantly and unhesitatingly expressing an uncompromising pathologic obsession for power and revenge: "What a moment this is! My prisoner thought that once he could destroy me. Now I shall twist the steel in his heart and shout 'triumph' in his ear as he dies."

Florestan is the hero of opera; his unfailing conscience prevented him from committing the sin of silence. He dared to speak the truth, and was willing to endanger his life for noble ideals. Act II opens with Florestan chained, alone, and despairing: "Gott! Welch' Dunkel hier!" ("God what darkness here! And what a deadly silence!") But he does not blame God for his suffering and fate: "My heart is comforted with the thought that I have done my duty. I accept the pain, I accept dying here in dishonor."

Beethoven was consumed by his belief that tragic drama must represent suffering as the highest achievement in life. As such, Florestan agonizes in despair and misfortune, just as the demon of deafness consumed the composer. But Leonore represents the elevating spirit — a sense of hope that perhaps Beethoven shared with his heroine as he confronted his deafness: "Ja, es gibt eine Vorsehung!" ("Yes, there is a Providence!")

Liberation, the final scene of *Fidelio*, echoes glorious human ideals: Leonore, the "eternal woman," succeeded after making sacrifices to rescue the man she loves; and the Minister Don Fernando dispenses justice and mercy for those suffering souls who have now been liberated from their tombs. As such, the music drama concludes with a profound vision: a sense of hope for humanity, and humanity's redemption as conflict transforms into reconciliation — an "Ode to Joy."

Fidelio is a "rescue opera." Beethoven identified with Florestan, unjustly imprisoned and depairing alone in his dark prison cell with no apparent hope of rescue; he was similarly filled with Florestan's pain and anguish, oppressed and isolated by the fate of his deafness. But it was the courage and fidelity of Leonore that rescued Florestan, just as Beethoven's muse, rescued him from the horror of deafness that overshadowed so much of his life.

In Wagner's prose, "Kuntswerk der Zukunft" ("Artwork of the Future"), the master opined that there was no greater ideal for the German musician than to express himself in the symphony; as such, he envisioned that Beethoven, a quintessential symphonist, must have suffered intensely after being confined and restrained by writing "music-pieces" for the opera *Fidelio* — vertually heartbroken by being restricted by musical forms from launching the full vitality and force of his expressive power. In essence, it was unfortunate that Beethoven had a limited opportunity to develop his musico-dramatic instincts; nevertheless, he sought to indemnify himself for that loss by throwing the entire weight of his genius into the Leonore Overtures, tone poems that aggressively anticipate so much of the opera's drama.

The Leonore Overtures emancipated Beethoven by enabling him to explain the drama in pure tonal form. In Leonore Overtures No. 2 and No. 3, Beethoven presents the dramatic elements with power and force, at times seemingly more completely and effectively than the entire music drama itself. As such, the Overtures capture the sufferings of the married lovers, the drama of Florestan's suffering, and the frenetic rejoicing at his rescue and reunion with Leonore. The climax of these Overtures is reached with the trumpet signal from the ramparts of the prison — the announcement of the approach of Don Fernando, the Minister. Leonore Overture No. 3 is based largely on the climactic first scene of Act II, Florestan's despairing aria, "Gott! Welch Dunkel hier!", and the trumpet flourishes that announce the approach of Don Fernando.

Beethoven wrote four overtures to *Fidelio*; at one time he contemplated another. The order of their composition has no specific dramatic logic: Leonore No. 2 was composed for the original production of 1805; Leonore No. 3, a revision of No. 2, was composed for the revival of 1806; Leonore No. 1, is a simplified adaptation of Nos. 2 and 3 that was composed for an 1806 Prague production that never materialized, and it features the music of Florestan's aria, "In des Lebens Frühlingstage," capturing the spirit of the dramatic action though not with the high tension of Leonore No. 2 and No. 3. It has been opined that No. 1 captures the happiness of the married lovers before the tragedy began, and therefore represents an excellent introduction to the opera.

The fourth overture is the *Overture to Fidelio,* a pure curtain raiser, lighter in dramatic texture than the three other Leonore Overtures. In comparison to Leonore Overtures Nos. 2, 3 and 4, it lacks a sense of epic majesty, vast symphonic structure, and highly dramatic narrative; it makes no use of melodic material employed in the opera and is more appropriately a true prelude built around unrelated musical ideas rather than a score that reflects moments of the whole drama. The *Overture to Fidelio* is considered a more appropriate introduction to the first scene of the opera, which serves to enable the listener to adapt to the domestic atmosphere of the first scene without difficulty.

Gustav Mahler introduced the practice of inserting Leonore Overture No. 3 between the scenes dividing Act II, although its inclusion at that point in the opera is dramatically incomprehensible, if only because its tumultuous final section sums up and rounds off the inner meaning of the drama with such overwhelming emotional power that the events of the final scene in which the Minister arrives can seem redundant. To many, the proper place for the Leonore Overtures is in the concert hall, not in the opera house.

Within he scope of the dramaturgy of *Fidelio,* Florestan is probably a man of about forty years. Leonore is a young Spanish woman of about twenty-five, her build conducive for her to wear a man's clothes without arousing any doubts as to her sex. As the curtain rises, the gravity of the ribald spectator is immediately tested: Leonore is dressed in man's clothes and must pass without suspicion as she performs daily labors in the jailer's household.

Unfortunately, however, the role of Leonore is that of a dramatic soprano, a demand for a powerful voice; in the real world she would more than likely be a soprano of mature age and of matronly build; it represents an appeal for an audience's politeness as they attempt to accept the character with credibility. The first great Fidelio, Wilhelmine Schröder-Devrient, was only eighteen in 1822 when she amazed the German music world with her combination of fine singing and acting in the role of Leonore.

To add a final touch of realism to the drama, there have been performances in which Leonore changes into woman's clothes for the final scene before the assembled crowd and the presence of the Minister, an idea that can provide greater impact to the praise of womanhood, as well as credibility to Marzelline's dismay and Rocco's astonishment at their discovery. This change of clothes can easily be accomplished because there is ample time that has elapsed before Florestan and Leonore appear after the change of scene from the dark dungeon to daylight.

There has been much skepticism and criticism about *Fidelio*'s first scene: that its domesticity would be more appropriate in a drama of less intensity. Nevertheless, Beethoven and his librettists intentionally invented these subsidiary characters: a second soprano (Marzelline, the daughter of the jailer) and a second tenor (Jaquino, her lover and wooer) who are far removed from the main tragic action. But ultimately, Marzelline and Jaquino provide charming domestic episodes that become superfluous to the intensity of the dramatic episodes that follow.

Fidelio represent is an opera possessing lofty ideals, an enduring metaphor for noble human aspirations that has become a beacon of hope for generations of people afflicted by oppression and tyranny. At its revival in 1814, at the Congress of Vienna meeting,the opera served to represent a protest against Napoleon. In 1937, a Toscanini performance in Salzburg intended to affirm the dignity of humanity as Hitler and the

Nazis awaited their conquest of Austria. In 1941, Bruno Walter conducted a series of Metropolitan Opera performances of *Fidelio* to express hope for the thousands of victims — like himself — who were escaping from Europe's Nazi terror. And after World War II, Furtwängler mounted *Fidelio* in Salzburg to symbolize his plea for reconciliation after the Nazi tyranny.

In 1954, after the death of Stalin in Soviet Russia, performances of *Fidelio* became a statement of outrage for those who were unjustly condemned to the regime's prisons. And when Vienna was liberated from the Soviet yolk in 1955, the reopened Staatsoper performed *Fidelio*, beaming it to listeners over loudspeakers — at times some became so emotionally overcome that they envisioned miracles being performed.

But *Fidelio* is also a testament to married love. In 1941, Kirsten Flagstad left America to join her husband in Norway, who had been a collaborator with the Nazis. But after the war she defended her actions by performing *Fidelio* as a testament to her love and heroism in remaining at her husband's side.

Ernest Newman commented on the universal ideals that saturate Beethoven's works: "Again and again (Beethoven) lifts us to a height from which we re-evaluate not only his music, but all life, all emotion, and all thought." Beethoven believed in noble ideals: equality, the brotherhood of humanity, the loving interdependence of man and woman, and the just providence of God.

But above all, Beethoven believed in the resilience of the human spirit in the face of oppression and tyranny. Those ideas remain at the core of *Fidelio*, Beethoven's sole opera. The opera endures because it represents a liberating experience; a story that ennobles the cornerstones of human aspirations — universal brotherhood, love, and compassion.

Principal Characters in Fidelio

Florestan, a Spanish nobleman	Tenor
Leonore, Florestan's wife, disguised as Fidelio (a young man)	Soprano
Rocco, jailer	Bass
Marzelline, Rocco's daughter	Soprano
Jaquino, Rocco's assistant, pursuing Marzelline	Tenor
Don Pizarro, governor of the prison, enemy of Florestan	Bass
Don Fernando, Minister of Spain, and friend of Florestan	Bass

Prisoners, guards, soldiers, people

TIME: Eighteenth century.

PLACE: Seville, Spain. A fortress for political prisoners.

Brief Story Synopsis

Fidelio is a singspiel, an opera in which the dramatic action and situations are explained by means of spoken dialogue and musical expositions.

The story takes place in Seville, Spain, during the eighteenth century. Two years before the curtain rises, Florestan, an official in the service of Don Fernando, Spain's Minister of State, mysteriously disappeared. Florestan is about forty-years-old, a man of lofty humanistic principles and ideals, and liberal political opinions. As such, he incurred the enmity of Don Pizarro, a reactionary, and governor of a state prison. Pizarro silenced Florestan by secretly commiting him to prison.

All believe that Florestan is dead, but his devoted wife, Leonore, doubts the official story; she has made it her consuming passion to find and rescue Florestan, hoping that he is still alive.

Leonore suspects that Florestan may be languishing in Pizarro's prison. She is a young Spanish woman of about twenty-five years, fortunate to have a slender build so that she could wear a man's clothes without arousing suspicions as to her sex. To search for Florestan in the prison, she enters the service of Rocco, the jailer, and disguises herself as a young man with the name of "Fidelio."

Fidelio proves his zeal and efficiency; Rocco regards him highly. Marzelline, his daughter, has fallen deeply in love with Fidelio, to the anguish of Jaquino, the young turnkey of the prison; until Fidelio's arrival, Jaquino had been pursuing Marzelline's love and harbored sincere hopes of marrying her.

Leonore discovers that Florestan is chained inside the dungeon, and that Pizarro plans to kill him before an imminent ministerial inspection of the prison. On Pzarro's orders, Rocco and Fidelio dig a grave for the prisoner. Just as Pizarro is about to murder Florestan, Leonore intervenes and identifies herself as Florestan's wife.

The Minister, Don Fernando, has learned of Pizarro's unjust imprisonment of Florestan and his attempt to murder him. Pizarro is arrested.

Leonore removes her husband's chains, and all celebrate their triumph over injustice — as well as the nobility of the conjugal love of Leonore and Florestan.

Story Narrative with Music Highlights

Overture to Fidelio:

An Allegro expresses a sense of joyous resolution.

A soft Adagio phrase succeeds the allegro.

After a repeat of the opening Allegro, another Adagio follows.

After pianissimo strings suggest the Adagio themes, the main Allegro of the Overture begins, a development of contrasting themes that express exhilaration and the triumph over injustice, oppression and tyranny. The finale of the Overture is a vociferous presto of the opening theme.

Unlike Leonore Overtures 1, 2 and 3, the *Overture to Fidelio* makes no reference to any music of the opera itself; its music merely suggests that the forces of good shall triumph over the forces of evil.

Act I: the courtyard of the prison

In the rear of the courtyard, there stands the gate of the main entrance, and a porter's lodge. On one side, there are prisoner's cells with heavily barred windows and bolted iron doors. The house of Rocco, the chief jailer, sits in the foreground.

Pizarro, the governor of the prison, has imprisoned Florestan, his political enemy. Florestan remains incognito and is chained in a secret dungeon.

Pizarro has spread a rumor that he died; but he is slowly starving Florestan to death.

The domestic ambience taking place in the courtyard of the prison is in sharp contrast to the gruesome horror within its walls. Marzelline, Rocco's daughter, is busy ironing at a table, while Jaquino, the jailer's assistant (turnkey), stands by the gate, every now and then admitting people carrying parcels for prisoners.

When Jaquino and Marzelline are alone, the young man becomes preoccupied in wooing her; he has become consumed by his hope and desire that they will marry.

Jetzt Schätzchen, jetzt sind wir allein

Jetzt, Schätzchen, jetzt sind wir allein, wir können vertraulich nun plaudern.

Jaquino and Marzelline were about to fix their wedding day, but she now resists him with a mixture of coquettish indifference and mild affection. Jaquino continues his childish and impetuous insistence and demands to know why she has suddenly become so aloof towards him. Marzelline becomes relieved when a knock at the door momentarily calls Jaquino to his duty.

Alone, Marzelline soliloquizes: she is sympathetic to Jaquino's affection for her, but since the young Fidelio has come to work at the prison as her father's assistant, she has suddenly become captivated; Marzelline has fallen in love with him young Fidelio (Leonore in a man's disguise.)

After Jaquino returns, he and renews his pursuit of Marzelline. She expresses her agitation and urges him to stop, but he is undaunted. Just as he is about to appeal to her again, Rocco is heard imperiously calling Jaquino to attend to people at the gate.

Alone again, Marzelline confesses her profound love for Fidelio: If only Fidelio would reciprocate her love? Would her father consent that she marry him?

Marzelline is now nursing dreams that perhaps one day she will marry Fidelio.

O wär' ich schon mit dir vereint

O wär' ich schon mit dir vereint, und dürf - te Mann dich nennen!

Rocco Jaquino arrive. Rocco inquires of Fidelio, wondering why he has not returned with the dispatches that he must soon present to the Governor. Marzelline offers her father the possible excuse that perhaps Fidelio was detained at the blacksmith.

As they speak there is a knocking at the door: Jaquino opens the door and admits Fidelio; it is Leonore, disguised as a young lad. (Leonore has become consumed to find her missing husband Florestan, and as Rocco's assistant, if Florestan is indeed one of the prisoners, she is convinced that she will find him. For her disguise, she wears dark knee breeches, a red waistcoat, boots, and a broad black leather belt with a copper buckle — her hair is swept back under a cap.

Fidelio's (Leonore) entrance:

Fidelio is heavily laden with purchases of supplies, and chains that were repaired by the blacksmith. Both Rocco and Marzelline help him unload. Rocco peruses the bill and then compliments the young man for buying with such thrift, but he attributes his zeal in his work to his desire to please his daughter, which causes Fidelio's embarrassment. While Rocco praises Fidelio, Marzelline gazes approvingly on the young man.

A Quartet begins, with each character expressing solemn and intense emotions. Marzelline begins: "How marvelous it is! My heart is about to burst! It is clear that he loves me."

Mir ist so wunderbar

Mir ist so wunderbar, es engt das Herz mir ein, er liebt mich, es ist klar,

Marzelline expresses her anxious dreams of a happy future with Fidelio; Fidelio becomes tormented, sensing that Marzelline's infatuation might endanger her purposes. Rocco observes Fidelio and assures Marzelline that they will be a happy couple; Jaquino becomes distraught, certain that his love for Marzelline will be doomed because Rocco will give his consent for her to marry Fidelio.

The Quartet is a canon in which each character sings the identical music. But each character expresses different sentiments: Marzelline (joy), Fidelio (foreboding), Rocco (optimism), and Jaquino (hopelessness). But it is Fidelio's suffering that is expressed with intensity in the grave music of the Quartet.

Rocco encourages the marriage of Marzelline and Fidelio; he enthusiastically announces that Fidelio shall become his son-in-law as soon as the Governor departs for his monthly trip to Seville to report on the condition of the State Prison.

Marzelline expresses her joy; Fidelio pretends happiness but is confounded. Rocco warns the young couple that love alone cannot bring happiness to a marriage — that a successful marriage must have money.

In the "Gold" aria, he expresses his philosophy.

Hat man nicht auch Gold

Hat man nicht auch Gold bei - ne-ben, kann man nicht ganz glück-lich sein;

Fidelio launches a plan of action that will enable her to gain admission to the subterranean dungeons so that she can determine if Florestan is among the prisoners. She convinces Rocco that he is overworked, always seemingly exhausted when he emerges from the vaults; if he has confidence in Fidelio, he should take advantage of his youthful vigor and allow him to accompany him. Marzelline further convinces her father, affectionately admonishing him that if he loves his children he must mind his health.

Rocco admits that he has been overworked. He tentatively agrees, but cautions that there is one cell in the secret dungeons into which only Rocco is allowed to enter; a cell in which a man has been imprisoned for two years. Fidelio becomes agitated and fearful, and struggles to control her emotions: "Did you say two years? He must be a great criminal!" Rocco replies, "Or he has powerful enemies, which amounts to much the same thing."

Marzelline inquires why it has never been possible to learn the prisoner's identity, or where he came from? Rocco reveals that the prisoner has often tried to speak with him, but in fear of his master, Governor Pizarro, he prudently closed his ears.

Rocco further reveals that Pizarro has ordered him to decrease the prisoner's daily rations; now, the prisoner has hardly any water or bread, and he is on the verge of death. Fidelio becomes shocked and horrified at Rocco's gruesome revelation. Marzelline pleads with her father that Fidelio should not descend into the dungeons with him; he fears that the sight would be unbearable. Fidelio refutes Marzelline with resolve and determination: "Why not? I am strong and courageous."

Rocco compliments Fidelio, "Well spoken, my son." It is the beginning of a trio in which Fidelio's resolution and grief become manifest. Fidelio declares that her boundless love will conquer her torment and anguish: she will pursue her noble duty, with fearless and unyielding determination.

Fidelio's (Leonore's) Resolution:

Allegro ma non troppo

In contrast, Marzelline exhorts Fidelio to think only of their love and future marriage. And Rocco assures the couple that because of his fading health, today he will ask the Governor's permission to share his work in the cells with his assistant, Fidelio.

The Trio concludes with Marzelline and Fidelio each addressing their tears: Marzelline speaks of "joyful tears"; and Fidelio expresses the anguish of her "bitter tears."

"O süsse Thrännen!" (Marzelline),
"O bitt're, bitt're Thränen!" (Fidelio)

Allegro ma non troppo

Don Pizarro, the Governor, arrives with officers and soldiers.

March, part 1:

March, part 2:

Jaquino opens the gate for the military entourage. Then, delivers a basket and the chains into Rocco's house. Fidelio hands Rocco the box of letters and then enters the house with Marzelline.

Pizarro brusquely orders sentries posted on the prison ramparts, the drawbridge, and at the garden-side of the walls: anyone approaching is to be brought before him at once. As he removes the letters from the box, he notices a letter with familiar handwriting — a letter from a friend in the Ministry. Pizarro reads the letter aloud: "For your information. It has come to the attention of the Minister that in the State prisons over which you preside there are several victims who are confined arbitrarily. The Governor begins his journey tomorrow for a surprise investigation. Be on your guard and protect yourself."

Pizarro becomes dismayed and overcome by fright: the Minister might discover that in revenge he imprisoned Florestan in chains; Florestan was a dear friend of the Minister whom he believes to be dead. Then Pizarro recovers his self-control: "There is but one escape for me. One bold deed can dispel all of my fears!"

In a furious outburst of revenge, Rocco expresses his hatred of Florestan, and his determination to seal his enemy's doom.

Ha! Ha! Ha' welch' ein Augenblick!

Men once mocked Pizarro, but now fate has endowed him with power: the power to destroy his enemies. Pizarro's tempestuous explosion of hatred and lust for blood injects fear in the listening soldiers. Pizarro has become crazed for revenge against those who have ridiculed and wronged him; his dagger in his victim's heart represents his triumph and vindication.

However, Pizarro must accomplish his vengeance against Florestan before the Minister arrives. He summons the Captain of the guard and orders him to post a trumpeter at the watchtower. He is to keep a vigil on the Seville road, and as soon as a carriage with cavalry escort approaches, the trumpeter must give a signal.

Pizarro calls to Rocco, aware that he needs the jailer's assistance to carry out his nefarious plans. Fidelio, unobserved, listens in on their conversation.

Pizarro informs Rocco that he is giving him the opportunity to become rich: he will pay the jailer handsomely if he helps him murder the prisoner Florestan. The jailer recoils in horror; he stammers and trembles. But Pizarro presses him hard, informing him that it is in the interests of the State to destroy this treacherous man. Pizarro remains undaunted, determined to engage the jailer's aid: "He must die or I am ruined; when he is dead I shall be safe." Rocco protests that murder is not part of his duties. Pizarro placates the nervous jailer: "If your courage fails you, I will perform the act." He orders Rocco to dig a grave in the old well of the dungeon; Pizarro himself will hide in the background, and when the grave is ready, he will come forth in disguise and kill the prisoner with his dagger.

Both speculate about the prisoner's imminent death: for Pizarro, Florestan's death will hide the truth of his unjust incarceration; for Rocco, the prisoner's death will be a merciful release from the poor man's interminable suffering at Pizarro's mercy.

After Rocco and Pizarro leave, Fidelio emerges. She has learned that a murder will be committed in the dungeons; as yet, she does not know for certain who the victim will be.

In an agitated recitative, she pours out her horror and loathing of Pizarro: "Abscheulicher! Wo eilst du hin? Was hast du vor? Was hast du vor in wildem Grimme?" ("Vile monster! What will you do? What drives you to such frantic passion?")

Fidelio then expresses her profound hope that love will guide and strengthen her to reach her goal.

Komm, Hoffnung lass den letzten Stern

Adagio
LEONORE

Komm,   Hoffnung lass den letzten Stern,   den letsten Stern der Müden nicht erbleichen,

Fidelio affirms her resolution to allow nothing to destroy her determination to find and rescue the man she loves.

Ich folg'dem innern Triebe

Marzelline and Jaquino exit the house. She admonishes the intrusive young man to cease complaining that she has been indifferent to him since Fidelio arrived. But she indeed admits that she loves Fidelio — and she is determined to marry him.

Fidelio returns with Rocco. Rocco inquires why Marzelline and Jaquino are quarreling. But Fidelio intervenes, and expresses her concern with more serious affairs. She begs Rocco to keep his promise and allow the prisoners to walk in the garden. Marzelline also presses her father, and since the Governor is not present, the jailer agrees to take the risk. Rocco orders Fidelio and Jaquino to open the cells.

Jaquino fetches the keys and Fidelio helps him unlock the prison doors. They leave the garden as the prisoners slowly and hesitantly emerge from their cells. They greet the daylight and fresh air with subdued expressions of exhilaration: "Oh, what joy! Released from gloom to breathe the reviving fresh air!"

O welche Lust!

The prisoners delight in the small mercy that has been granted them, but they also express their fears of the hostile guards. Fidelio scrutinizes the prisoners but fails to find Florestan.

Rocco enters the garden with good news: Pizarro not only sanctions the marriage of Fidelio and Marzelline, but consents to Fidelio being allowed to descend into the dungeon with the jailer that very day. The news causes Fidelio to impulsively erupt into joy. Rocco explains that the work they must perform in the dungeons is urgent.

He announces that the mysterious prisoner is dying; he has been given less and less to eat and therefore they must prepare a grave for him. Apprehensively, Fidelio inquires if he is dead? Rocco replies, "Not yet, not yet." Fidelio inquires fearfully: "Are you going to kill him, then?" The jailer reassures her that he himself will not commit murder, but that the Governor himself will meet them in the dungeon and strike the fatal blow; their duty is only to prepare the grave.

Fidelio weeps, causing Rocco to be apprehensive whether the lad is able to cope with the gruesome work of digging the grave. He offers to spare him the ordeal and carry out Pizarro's orders alone. But Fidelio hides the emotions that torment her, and protests that she must heed her duty.

Marzelline and Jaquino arrive to announce that Pizarro is enraged after learning from an officer of Rocco's compassion for the prisoners. Suddenly, Pizarro and officers storm through the gate, the Governor cursing the jailer for his brashness. Rocco calms Pizarro with a crafty excuse: that he surely could permit an indulgence on the King's name-day; let the Governor spare his rage for the one prisoner who has remained below.

Pizarro orders Rocco to go below at once and dig the grave. Meanwhile the prisoners return to their cells, lamenting the brevity of their moment of light and air.

Leb'wohl, du warmes Sonnenlicht, schnell

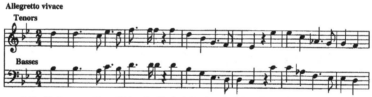

Leb'wohl, du warmes Sonnenlicht, schnell schwindest du uns wieder, schnell schwindest du uns wieder,

Pizarro repeats his frenzied command that Rocco go below and perform his duty. The jailer becomes heavy-hearted and trembles, but he dare not refuse. Fidelio observes the sinister Pizarro and wonders if justice has vanished from heaven; Marzelline expresses her sympathy for the downtrodden prisoners as they are cowed back to their cells; Jaquino is oblivious to the prisoner's misery, his heart so full of his blind jealousy of Fidelio; and Pizarro continues to seethe with revenge.

The first act concludes amid heightened tension, with somber chords in the orchestra forecasting a apprehension and gloom.

Act II

Florestan is imprisoned is a dark and bleak subterranean dungeon; he is seated on a stone and fastened to the wall by a chain.

The sense of gloom in Florestan's living tomb is conveyed by a somber orchestral introduction, an anguished chromatic phrase with tremolandos in the strings played over throbbing beats of the kettledrums.

Florestan begins a poignant monologue that describes his grievous state: "Gott! Welch Dunkel hier!" ("God! What darkness here!")

Gott! Welch Dunkel hier!

Florestan recalls his former youth and freedom, but welcomes death, a tragic fate that he accepts as God's will. He is innocent of any crime: he loved liberty and was noble, and dared to speak the truth — but chains and endless torment have become his reward.

In der Lebens Frühlingstagen

Florestan becomes ecstatic when he imagines fresh air filling his cell. Does he see a light? He imagines it is a radiant angel: Leonore rescuing him and bringing him to freedom in a new and better world.

Ein Engel Leonoren

Florestan sinks, exhausted; he hides his face in his hands.

Rocco and Fidelio descend the prison stairway: they carry a lantern, a pitcher, and tools for digging. Rocco points out the almost invisible form of Florestan. Fidelio seeks to catch a glimpse of the prisoner's face, but in the darkness she is unable to determine his features: "God help me if it is him!"

Rocco descends into the abandoned cistern and begins digging. Fidelio trembles from the cold; Rocco urges her to work to keep warm. They must work fast and with great effort because the Governor will be arriving soon. As Rocco digs, Fidelio continues to scrutinize the prisoner.

Ihr sollt ja nicht zu klagen haben

Andante con moto
LEONORE

Ihr sollt ja   nicht zu kla - gen   ha-ben,Ihr sollt ge - wiss   zufrie - den sein.

Together they dislodge a heavy stone from the pit. As the grisly work continues, Fidelio anxiously scans the face of the sleeping prisoner. She is uncertain of his identity but feels intense pity for the man; she heroically vows that whoever he may be, she will somehow loosen his chains and rescue him.

As Rocco pauses in his work for a drink of wine, Fidelio becomes extremely agitated when she observes that the prisoner has awakened. Rocco emerges from the pit to approach the prisoner, certain that he will be asked a thousand questions. He must speak with him alone. Fidelio is ordered to leave, Rocco alone with the prisoner.

Rocco inquires of the prisoner if he has rested. Florestan replies: "Rest? Where could I ever find rest?" Although his voice is faint, Fidelio thinks she recognizes it: "If only I could see his face for a moment!" While the prisoner reproaches his jailer for his harshness, he turns his face in the direction of Fidelio, who recognizes Florestan; she faints at the edge of the grave.

Florestan inquires why Rocco never listens to his complaints. Rocco defends himself as a man who performs his duty by obeying orders. Florestan inquires: Who is the Governor of this prison? Rocco replies that it is Don Pizarro. Florestan becomes anguished: "Pizarro! The very man whose crimes I exposed." As Fidelio gradually regains consciousness, Florestan urges Rocco to send someone as quickly as possible to Seville to find Leonore, the wife of Florestan, and tell her that he her husband is imprisoned here in chains — in the power of the cruel Pizarro.

Fidelio murmurs: "Oh God! If he knew that I am here digging his grave!" Florestan pleads with Rocco not to let him die of starvation and requests some water. All that Rocco can offer him is what is left of the wine in his pitcher, which he orders Fidelio to bring to him. Fidelio rushes to Florestan's side with the wine and cries our ecstatically, "Here it is!"

Florestan offers heartfelt thanks to the merciful young man for the refreshment.

Euch werde Lohn in bessern Welten

Fidelio finds Florestan's suffering unbearable. She is overcome by both hope and fear, but realizes that she must rescue him or he will die. Florestan observes the young lad, commenting how emotional he has become. Fidelio takes a piece of bread from her pocket and convinces Rocco, who has pity for the man, to allow her to give it to him. In extreme agitation, Fidelio gives Florestan the bread, which he seizes from her hand. He thanks her profusely.

Da nimm, da dimm das Brod

Rocco decides to give Pizarro the signal; he goes to the rear, opens the door, and blows a shrill whistle. Florestan murmurs: "Is that the signal for my death? Oh, my Leonore! Shall I ever see you again?" Fidelio attempts to master her emotions, and then urges him to be calm: "Be calm, I tell you. Remember, whatever you may see and hear, there is Providence!"

As Pizarro enters the dungeon, disguised by his cloak, Fidelio returns to hide by the well. In a sinister undertone, Pizarro inquires of Rocco if everything is ready? Rocco gives his assurance. Pizarro orders Rocco to dismiss Fidelio; she retires to the background. Pizarro mutters to himself that to secure his own safety he must kill the prisoner as well as the jailer. Rocco is about to unchain Florestan from the stone when Pizarro stops him. He draws his dagger and erupts into another ferocious denunciation of his victim: "He shall die here! But before, I will reveal who vanquishes him." Pizarro throws back his cloak and reveals himself to Florestan, furiously repeating that his day of revenge has finally arrived.

Overcome and blind with fury, Pizarro is about to stab the defenseless Florestan, but Fidelio rushes forward and defiantly shields Florestan with her body: "Zurük!" ("Back! You'll first plunge the dagger into my breast. I've vowed death for you, you murderer!")

Rocco urges Fidelio to stand back out of harm's way. In a burst of rage Pizarro attempts to kill both. But Fidelio is in complete control of the situation. Defiantly, she reveals her identity in a dramatic outburst: "Tödt'erst sein Weib!" ("First kill his wife!")

All are stunned. Leonore proudly tells them: "Yes, it is Leonore! I am his wife! I've sworn to avenge his wrongs, and undermine your will!" As Pizarro is about to challenge Leonore, she draws a pistol and points it at him.

A trumpet fanfare is heard, the warning from the tower that the Minister's cortege has been sighted on the Seville road.

Trumpet fanfare:

Florestan and Leonore embrace as they celebrate their reunion and pour out their gratitude.

Pizarro and Rocco remain stunned at the unexpected turn of events. The trumpet signal rings out again. Jaquino, officers and soldiers appear at the stairway, Jaquino announcing that the Minister and his entourage are already at the gates.

In a vigorous quartet, Leonore and Florestan express gratitude that their hour of vengeance has arrived; Pizarro invokes curses on those who have scorned him; and Rocco is torn between fear and relief that he will no longer serve as the reluctant instrument of Pizarro's cruel will. The torchbearers escort Pizarro and exit, Rocco following them.

Leonore and Florestan fall into each other's arms. Florestan emotionally calls to his wife: "O my Leonore!" Leonore responds: "Florestan!" Florestan inquires: "Was hast du für mich gethan?" ("What have you done for me?") Leonore replies nobly: "Nichts, mein Florestan!" ("Nothing, my Florestan!")

In an ecstatic and rapturous duet, they pour out their gratitude to heaven for the grace that has been granted them.

O namen, namenlose Freude!

In the courtyard of the prison, Marzelline, Jaquino, the prisoners, and an exuberant crowd of townspeople have assembled to greet Don Fernando, the benevolent Minister of State. Fernando arrives with Pizarro, the latter escorted by a guard. All praise the new day of justice that has dawned.

Majestically, the Minister expounds his sentiments about the injustices that had befallen them: "I have come at the will of our King to learn of your pain. I will bring light to your darkness, and lift the veil of foul misdeed. No longer kneel in slavish fear. I fulfill no tyrant's mandate. Let brother seek brother, and help wherever he can."

The crowd praises the Minister's sentiments enthusiastically.

Rocco forces his way through the guards, accompanied by Leonore and Florestan. He suggests to the Minister that the couple is especially worthy of his compassion: the victims of tyranny and oppression. Don Fernando is astonished to recognize that the broken man standing before him in chains is Florestan, his old friend, who had fought so nobly for humanity, and whom he had long thought dead; he is even more astonished at the sight of Leonore in the prison.

Rocco explains that Leonore had come to work for him in male disguise; her noble purpose was to rescue her husband. She had served as his assistant. She was so scrupulous in the performance of his duties that he had accepted him as his future son-in-law. The disclosure of Fidelio's sex fills poor Marzelline with confusion and dismay. The jailer points to Pizarro and condemns him for planning to murder Florestan, a deed that was prevented only by the timely arrival of the Minister. The people demand that Pizarro be punished. Fernando orders Pizarro arrested, and soldiers remove him.

But the Minister takes a lenient view of Rocco's complicity. He is about to command Rocco to remove Florestan's chains, but decides that the privilege belongs to his noble wife. Leonore takes the key and unlocks Florestan's chains; he sinks into her arms. Florestan voices his happiness, Fernando praises the justice of heaven, Marzelline and Rocco echo him, and the townspeople give thanks to God.

There is a hymn of praise to the valor of Leonore, the noble wife: "Let all who have won for themselves a gracious wife join in our jubilant song."

Wer ein holdes Weib errungen

There is universal rejoicing, but particular praise to the glory of married love; and to Leonore, the noble woman who risked her life to rescue her husband, Florestan.

Libretto

Act I — Music Highlight Index

Duet:Jaquino, Marzelline (P 45)
Jetzt, Schätzchen, jetz sind wir allein

Aria: Marzelline (P 49)
O wär' ich schon mit dir vereint

Quartet: Marzelline, Fidelio (Leonore), Rocco, Jaquino (P 51)
Mir ist so wunderbar

Aria: Rocco (P 52)
Hat man nicht auch Gold beineben

Trio: Rocco, Marzelline, Fidelio (Leonore) (P 55)
Gut, Söhnchen, gut!

Aria: Pizarro, Soldiers (P 58)
Ha! Welch' ein Augenblick!

Duet: Pizarro, Rocco (P 59)
Jetzt, Alter, jetzt hat es Eile!

Aria: Leonore (P 61)
Abscheulicher! Wo eilst du hin?

Chor der Gegangenen (P 64)
O welche Lust, in freier Luft

Quintet, Chorus (Page 67)
Ach, Vater, Vater, eilt!

Act I

The Courtyard of a State Prison. In the garden, Marzelline is ironing linens. Jacquino attends the gate door, which he opens for persons delivering parcels for prisoners.

Duet: Jaquino, Marzelline

Jaquino:
Jetzt, Schätzchen, jetz sind wir allein,
wir können vertraulicht nun plaudern.

Jaquino:
At last, my idol, we are alone,
and we can have a pleasant chat together.

Marzelline:
Es wird ja nichts wichtiges sein;
ich darf beider Arbeit nicht zaudern.

Marzelline:
Well, speak away, but don't annoy me:
I have my work to do, you know.

Jaquino:
Ein Wörtchen, du Trotzige du!

Jaquino:
A word with you—just a word.

Marzelline:
So sprich nur! Ich höre ja zu.

Marzelline:
Go on; I'm listening.

Jaquino:
Wenn du mir nicht freundlicher blickest,
so bring' ich kein Wörtchen hervor.

Jaquino:
But, at least, do not be cross with me,
or I shall not be able to say a word.

Marzelline:
Wenn du dich nicht in mich schickest,
ver stopf' ich mir vollends das Ohr.

Marzelline:
Well, and when you do speak,
perhaps I shall close my ears.

Jaquino:
Ein Weilchen nur höre mir zu,
Dann lass ich dich wieder in Ruh.

Jaquino:
Only listen for a few moments,
and then I'll leave you in peace.

Marzelline:.
So ich habe denn nimmermehr Ruh.
So rede, so rede nur zu.

Marzelline:
You are always tormenting me.
I am listening, speak on.

Jaquino:
Ich habe zum Weib dich gewählet.
Verstehst du?

Jaquino:
I have chosen you for my wife.
Do you understand?

Marzelline:.
Das ist ja doch klar!

Marzelline:
Yes, that's plain enough!

Jaquino:
Und wenn mir dein Jawort nich fehlet,
Was meinst du?

Jaquino:
And if you would only say yes,
what then?

Marzelline:.
So sind wir ein Paar.

Marzelline:
Why, then we would make a pair.

Jaquino:
Wir könnten in wenigen Wochen—

Jaquino:
In a week or two, we could—

Marzelline:.
Recht schön! Du bestimmst schon die Zeit.

Marzelline:
Well done! You are certainly fixing an early time.

There is a knocking on the door.

Jaquino:
Zum Henker! Das ewige Pochen!

Jaquino:
The deuce! That eternal knocking!

Marzelline:.
So bin ich doch endlich befreit!

Marzelline: *(aside)*
For the present I am saved.

Jaquino:
Da war ich so herrlich im Gang.

Jaquino:
I was just getting on the right track.

Marzelline:.
Wie macht seine Liebe mir bang.

Marzelline:
How uneasy he makes me.

Jaquino:
Und immer entwischt mir der Fang!

Jaquino:
But the prize always escapes me.

Marzelline:
Wie werden die Stunden mir lang.
Ich weiss, dass der Arme sich quälet,
Es thut mir so leid auch um ihn;
Fidelio! Hab' ich gewählet,
Ihn lieben ist süsser Gewinn.

Marzelline:
How slowly the time seems to pass.
I know this poor fellow suffers,
and I am rightfully sorry for him.
But Fidelio has my heart,
and his love is the only treasure I value.

Jacquino:
Wo war ich? Sie sieht mich nich an.

Jaquino:
Where was I? She turns her back upon me.

Marzelline:
Da ist er, er fängt wieder an.

Marzelline:
There he is—going on again.

Jaquino:
Wann wirst du das Jawort mir geben?
Es könnte ja heute noch sein.

Jaquino:
Oh, when will you say "Yes" to me?
Why not do so today?

Marzelline:
O weh! Er verbittert mein Leben!
Jetzt—morgen—und immer—nein, nein!

Marzelline:
Oh, woe's me! He's a constant torment!
Once, always, and forever, I say no, no!

Jaquino:
Du bist doch wahrhaftig von Stein.

Marzelline:
Ich muss ja so hart mit ihm sein.

Jaquino:
Kein Wünschen, kein Bitten geht ein.

Marzelline:
Er hofft bei dem mindesten Schein.

Jaquino:
So wirst du dich nimmer bekehren?
Was meinst du?

Marzelline:
Du könntest nun gehn.

Jaquino:
Wie? Dich anzusehn willst du mir
wehren? Auch das noch?

Marzelline:
So bleibe hier stehn.

Jaquino:
Du hast mir so oft doch versprochen—

Marzelline:
Versprochen? Nein! Das geht zu weit!

Jaquino:
Then you must have a heart of stone.

Marzelline: *(aside)*
I must be harsh with him.

Jaquino:
Will vows or prayers move you?

Marzelline:
My least giving way gives him hope.

Jaquino:
Will you ever relent?
Speak—what do you say?

Marzelline:
That you go.

Jaquino:
What! Must I quit while in your sight?
May I not even look on you?

Marzelline:
Well, then stay and stand there.

Jaquino:
But how often you have promised—

Marzelline:
Promised? No! That's going too far!

The knocking at the door continues.

Jaquino:
Zum Henker! das ewige Pochen!

Marzelline:
So bin ich doch endlich befreit.

Jaquino:
Es ward ihr im Ernste schon bang,

Marzelline:
Das war ein willkommener Klang!

Jaquino:
Wer weiss ob es mir nicht gelang?

Jaquino:
The deuce! That eternal knocking!

Marzelline:
At last I shall be left at peace.

Jaquino:
She begins to relent a little, I think.

Marzelline: *(aside)*
Oh, what a welcome sound!

Jaquino:
Who knows if I succeeded?

Marzelline:
Es wurde zu Tode mir bang.

Jaquino:
Wenn ich diese Thüre heute nicht schon zweihundertmal aufgemacht, so will ich nicht Jaquino heissen.

Endlich kann ich doch einmal wieder plaudern.
Zum Wetter! Schon wieder!

Marzelline:
Was kann ich dafür, dass ich ihn nicht mehr so gern haben kann, wie sonst?

Jaquino:
Schon recht! Ich werde es besorgen. So. Nun hoffe ich, soll Niemand uns stören.

Rocco:
Jaquino! Jaquino!

Marzelline:
Hörst du! Der Vater ruft.

Jaquino:
Lassen wir ihn ein wenig warten. Also wieder auf unsere Liebe zu kommen.

Marzelline:
So geh doch! Der Vater wird sich nach Fidelio erkundigen wollen.

Jaquino:
Ei, freilich! Da kann man nicht schnell genug sein.

Rocco:
Jaquino! Hörst du nicht?

Jaquino:
Ich komme schon! Bleib' hier; in zwei Minuten sind wir wieder beisammen.

Marzelline:
I'm dying from anxiety.

Jaquino:
If I have not answered that door two hundred times today, my name's not Caspar Eustache Jaquino.
(to Marzelline)
At last we are at liberty to speak freely.
(knocking)
The deuce! again knocking!
(Jaquino opens the door)

Marzelline:
What shall I do? I don't even love him as I used to.

Jaquino: *(to the person knocking)*
That will do; I will attend to the door. Now I hope we have no more disturbers.

Rocco: *(calling)*
Jaquino! Jaquino!

Marzelline:
Do you not hear? My father calls.

Jaquino:
Well, let him wait a bit, while we finish our love affairs.

Marzelline:
No, no; go! Father may be wishing to enquire after Fidelio.

Jaquino: *(with jealousy)*
Oh, truly! and in that case one cannot be quick enough.

Rocco: *(calling again)*
Jaquino! Don't you hear me?

Jaquino: *(to Marzelline)*
Do not go now, I pray to you—in two minutes I shall be back again.

Marzelline:
Der arme Jaquino dauert mich beinahe.
Kann ich es aber ändern? Ich warihm
sonst recht gut, da kam Fidelio in under
Haus, und seit ist alles in mir und um
mich verändert.

Aria: Marzelline
O wär' ich schon mit dir vereint, und
dürfte Mann dich nennen! Ein Mädchen
darf ja, was es meint, zur Hälfte nur
bekennen. Doch wenn ich nicht erröthen
muss, ob einem warmen Herzenskuss,
Wenn nichts uns stört au Erden. Die
Hoffnung schon erfüllt die Brust Mit
unaussprechlich süsser Lust!

Wie glücklich will ich werden. In Ruhe
stiller Häuslichkeit, erwach ich jeden
Morgen; Wir grüssen uns mit
Zärtlichkeit. Der Fleiss verscheucht die
Sorgen. Und ist die Arbeit abgethan,
Dann schleicht die holde Nacht heran,
Dann ruh'n wir von Beschwerden. Die
Hoffnung schon erfüllt die Brust Mit
unaussprechlich süsser Lust! Wie
glücklich will ich werden!

Rocco:
Guten Tag, Marcelline! Ist Fidelio noch
nicht rurückgekommen?

Marzelline:
Nein, Vater!

Rocco:.
Die Stunde naht, wo ich dem Gouverneur die
Briefschaften bringen muss, die Fidelo abholen
sollte. Ich erwarte ihn mit Ungeduld.

Jaquino:
Ich komme schon! Ich komme schon!

Marzelline:
Er wird gewiss so lange bei dem
Schmiede haben worten müssen.

Da ist er ja! Da ist er!

Marzelline:
Poor Jaquino! I feel so sorry for him. But
how can I change it? I really used to like
him; then Fidelio came into our house,
and since then, everything within and
without me has changed.

Oh, if I were already united with you,
what should I call you! A maiden could
confess to only half of what she thinks.
But I do not have to blush, from a warm
kiss of the heart. If nothing bothers us on
earth, hope already fills the breast,
with unspeakably sweet lust,
How happy will I become!

How happy I want to be. In a quiet
domestic life, when I awaken every
morning. We greet each other with
tenderness. The work scares away the
worries. And when the work is finished,
the fair night sneaks in.
Then we rest from complaints.
Hope already fills the breast,
with unspeakably sweet lust.
How happy will I become!

Rocco:
Good day, Marzelline! Has Fidelio
returned yet?

Marzelline:
No, father!

Rocco:
The time has come for me to deliver to
the packet of letters that Fidelio fetched,
to the Governor.

Jaquino: *(rushes to unlock the door)*
Coming, coming!

Marzelline:
Perhaps he was obliged to wait at the
smith.
(Seeing Fidelio - Leonore - at the door.)
Why, here he is, here he is!

Fidelio enters. She (Leonore) carries a basket with provisions. There are fetters on her arms. At her side is a tin box, hanging by a ribbon!

Marzelline:
Wie er belastet ist. Liebe Gott! Der Schweiss läuft ihm von der Stirne.

Marzelline: *(rushing to Fidelio)*
So heavy! Good heavens! the perspiration streams from his forehead.

Rocco:
Warte! warte!

Rocco:
Oh, stay, stay!

Jaquino:
Es war auch wohl der Mühe werth, so schnell zu laufen, um den Patron da hereinzulassen.

Jaquino: *(aside)*
It was worth the trouble, certainly, to run so quickly to let my gentleman in!

Rocco:
Armer Fidelio! Diesmal hast du dir zu viel aufgeladen.

Rocco:
My poor Fidelio! This time you have somewhat overladen yourself.

Leonore:.
Ich muss gestehen, ich ben ein wenig ermüdet.

Leonore:
I must confess, this time I'm a little wearied.

Rocco:.
Wieviel kostet Alles zusammen?

Rocco:
How much did these things cost?

Leonore:
Zwölf Piaster ohngefähr. Hier ist die genaue Rechnung.

Leonore:
About twelve piastres; here is the accounting.

Rocco:.
Gut! brav! Zum Wetter! Da giebt es Artikel, auf die man wenigstens das Doppelte profitiren kann. Du bist ein kluger Junge! Der Schelm giebt sich alle diese Mühe offenbar meiner Marzelline wegen.

Rocco:
Good! capital! By all that's good, here are articles by which we shall at least make a profit.
The rogue plainly gives himself all this trouble because of my Marzelline.

Leonore:
Ich suche zu thun, was mir möglich ist.

Leonore:
I wish to do all I can.

Rocco:.
Ja, ja! Du bist brav! Ich habe dich aber auch mit jedem Tage lieber; und sey versichert, dein Lohn soll nicht ausbleiben.

Rocco:
Yes, yes, you art a good fellow! I like you better and better, and be assured you shall receive your reward.

Leonore:
O glaubt nicht, dass ich meine Schuldigkeit nur des Lohnes wegen.

Leonore: *(embarrassed)*
Oh! Don't think that I do my duty from uninterested motives.

Rocco:.
Still! Meinst du ich kann dir nicht ins
Herz schen?

Rocco:
Be still! do you think that I cannot see
into your heart?

Quartet: Marzelline, Fidelio (Leonore), Rocco, Jaquino

Marzelline:
Mir ist so wunderbar,
Es engt das Herz mir ein;
Er liebt mich, es ist klar,
Ich werde glücklich sein.

Marzelline:
I have such a strange feeling,
that tightly grips my heart.
He loves me, it is clear,
and I shall be happy with him.

Leonore:
Wie gross ist die Gefahr,
Wie schwach der Hoffnung Schein!
Sie liebt mich, es ist klar,
O namenlose Pein!

Leonore:
How great the danger is;
how weak the rays of hope!
She loves me, it is clear;
my sufferings never end.

Rocco:.
Sie liebt ihn, es ist klar;
Ja, Mädchen, er wird dein. Ein gutes,
junges Paar,
Sie werden glücklich sein.

Rocco:
She loves him, it is clear;
Yes, girl, he will be yours.
A couple, young and good,
shall be happy together.

Jaquino:
Mir sträubt sich schon das Haar,
Der Vater willigt ein;
Mir wird so wunderbar,
Mir fällt kein Mittel ein.

Jaquino:
My hair stands on end.
The father will consent;
I've never known the feeling,
and there's nothing I can do.

Der Vater willigt ein,
Mir wird so wunderbar,
Mir fällt kein Mittel ein.

They share Rocco's blessing,
What wondrous, and strange things
for which I can do nothing!

Rocco:
Höre, Fidelio, wenn ich auch nicht weiss,
wem du angehörst, so weiss ich doch, was
ich thue; ich—ich mache dich zu meinem
Tochtermann.

Rocco:
Well, my good Fidelio, I do not know
who you are, and I know not what I am
doing. But I'll accept you as my son-in-
law.

Marzelline:
Wirst du es bald thun, Vater?

Marzelline:
Will you? Soon, father?

Rocco:
Ei, ei, wie eilfertig! Sobald der Gouverneur
nach Sevilla gereis't seyn wird, dann geb' ich
Euch zusammen: darauf könnt Ihr rechnen.

Rocco:
Oh, oh, what a hurry! As soon as the
Governor has set out for Seville I will
unite you; on that you may depend.

Marzelline:.
Den Tag nach seiner Abreise? Das machst du recht vernünftig, lieber Vater.

Marzelline:
You mean the day after his departure? Dear father, you are quite right.

Leonore:
Den Tag nach seiner Arbreise?

O, welche neue Verlegenheit!

Leonore: *(embarrassed, but joyful)*
The day after his departure? [*(aside)*
What new troubles must I encounter?

Rocco:
Nun, meine Kinder, Ihr habt Euch doch herzlich lieb, nicht wahr? Aber das ist noch nicht Alles was zu einer vegnügten Haushaltung gehört, man braucht auch.

Rocco:
Now, my children, you truly love one another; do I not see that?
But there are other needs to make housekeeping agreeable!

Aria: Rocco

Hat man nicht auch Gold beineben,
Kann man nicht ganz glücklich sein;
Traurig schleppt sich fort das Leben,
Mancher Kummer stellt sich ein.
Doch wenn's in den Taschen fein klingelt und rollt,
Da hält man das Schicksal gefangen,
und Macht und Liebe verschafft dir das Gold und stillet das kühnste Verlangen.
Das Glück dient wie ein Knecht für Sold,
Your luck serves like a serf for pay,
Es ist ein schönes Ding, das Gold.

Unless there is gold to live on,
you will never be quite happy.
Sadly life will carry on,
but many a sorrow will set in.
But if it tinkles and rolls in the pockets,
fate will have you at its mercy.
Gold will keep fate trapped; it will provide you with power and love,
and it will still your boldest desires.
Gold can serve you well: happiness serves as a servant for pay; luck serves as a serf for pay. With gold, you pay for luck, it is a wonderful thing.

Wenn sich Nichts mit Nichts verbindet,
Ist und bleibt die Summe klein;
Wer bei Tisch nur Liebe findet,
Wird nach Tische hungrig sein.
Drum lächle der Zufall euch gnädig und hold,
Und segne und lenk' euer Streben;
Das Liebchen im Arme,
im Beutel das Gold.

When nothing connects with nothing,
the sum remains small; one who finds love only at a table, one will be hungry afterwards.
So may fortune be gracious and kind,
and bless and guide your striving.
With your beloved at your side, gold in your purse, you'll have many years of happiness. Gold is a mighty thing.

Leonore:
Ihr könnt das leicht sagen. Meister Rokko. Freilich giebt es noch etwas, was mir nicht minder kostbar seyn würde; aber mit Kummer sehe ich, dass ich es durch alle miene Bemühungen nicht erhalten werde.

Leonore:
You can say that easily, Master Rocco. Of course there is something else that would not be less precious to me; but with sorrow I see that I will not receive it through all my efforts; with sorrow I perceive all my exertions cannot gain.

Rocco:
Und was wäre denn das?

Rocco:
And what is that?

Leonore:
Euer Vertrauen. Verzeiht mir den
Vorwurf, aber oft sehe ich Euch aus den
unterirdischen Gewölben dieses
Schlosses ganz ausser Athem und
ermattet zurückkommen.
Warum erlaubt Ihr mir nicht Euch dahin
zu begleiten. Es wäre mir sehr lieb, wenn
ich Euch bei Eurer Arbeit helfen und Eure
Beschwerden theilen könnte.

Leonore:
Your confidence! Pardon me for
reproaching you, but I often see you
returning from the subterranean vaults of
the castle, and you are quite out of
breath.
Why don't you allow me to accompany
you? It would be a delight for me
if I could go with you, and share your
toils.

Rocco:
Du weisst doch, dass ich den strengsten
Befehl habe, Niemanden, wer's auch sey,
zu den Staats-Gefangenen zu lassen.

Rocco:
But you know the strict orders imposed
on me. I am forbidden to allow access to
any one of the state prisoners.

Marzelline:
Es sind ihrer aber gar zu viele in dieser
Festung. Du arbeitest dich ja zu Tode,
liebe Vater.

Marzelline:
But there are far too many of them in
this fortress. And, dear father, you would
work yourself to death.

Leonore:
Sie hat recht, Meister Rokko. Man soll
allerdings seine Pflicht thun, aber ist doch
auch erlaubt, mein ich, zuweilen daran zu
denken, wie man sich für die, welche uns
angehören und lieben, ein Bischen
schonen kann.

Leonore: *(grasping Rocco's hand)*
She is right, Master Rocco.
One must certainly do one's duty,
and it is allowable, I believe,
to spare oneself a little energy
for those who belong to us,
and for those who love us.

Marzelline:
Man muss sich für seine Kinder zu
erhalten suchen.

Marzelline:
One must try, for the sake of one's
children.

Rocco:
Ja, Ihr abt recht! Diese schwere Arbeit
würde mir doch endlich zu viel werden.
Der Gouverneur ist zwar sehr streng; er
muss mir aber doch erlauben, dich in die
geheimen Kerker mit mir zu nehmen.

Rocco: *(affected)*
Well said, my children: this hard work is
becoming too much for me. The
Governor, it is true, is very strict; but in
time he should allow me to take you with
me into the secret dungeons.

Indessen giebst es ein Gewölbe, in das ich dich
wohl nie werde einführen dürfen, obschon ich
mich ganz auf dich verlassen kann.

(Fidelio becomes joyful)
However, there is one dungeon,
Fidelio, and I am not permitted to take
you into it.

Marzelline:
Verrumthlich wo der Gefangene sitzt, von dem du schon einigemal gesprochen hast, Vater.

Marzelline:
Probably that is there the prisoner is confined, the one you have often spoken about, father?

Rocco:
Du hast's errathen.

Rocco:
You guessed it.

Leonore:
Ich glaube, es ist schon lange her, dass er gefangen ist?

Leonore: *(inquiringly)*
I think he has been imprisoned here a very long time?

Rocco:
Es ist schon über zwei Jahr.

Rocco:
Somewhat more than two years.

Leonore:
Zwei Jahr, sagt Ihr? Er muss ein grosser Verbrecher seyn.

Leonore: *(impetuously)*
Two years, do you say?
Then he must be a dangerous criminal?

Rocco: .
Oder er muss grosse Feinde haben: dieses kommt ohngefähr auf eins heraus.

Rocco:
Or he must have great enemies: that amounts to the same thing.

Marzelline:
So hat man denn nie erfahren können, woher er ist und wie er heisst?

Marzelline:
Is no one able to tell his name, or from where he comes?

Rocco: .
O wie oft hat er mit mir von alle dem sprechen wollen!

Rocco:
Oh how often he has wished to speak with me of his past!

Leonore:
Nun?

Leonore:
Well?

Rocco:
Für Unsereinen ist's aber am besten, so wenig Geheimnisse, als möglich zu wissen.Nun, er wird mich nicht lange mehr quälen, es kann nicht mehr lange mit ihm dauern.

Rocco: *(mysteriously)*
For people in our position,
it is best to know as few secrets as possible. However, he will not trouble me much more since he cannot last much longer.

Leonore: .
Grosser Gott!

Leonore: *(aside)*
Great God!

Marzelline:
O lieber Vater, führe Fidelio ja nicht zu ihm; diesen Anblick könnte er nicht ertragen.

Marzelline:
Do not take Fidelio to him, father dear: it is a sight he could not bear.

Leonore:
Warum denn nicht? Ich habe Muth und
Stärke!

Leonora:
Oh! fear me not. Do not doubt my
courage or my strength!

Rocco:
Brav! mein Sohn! brav! Wenn ich dir
erzählen wollte, wie ich anfangs in
meinem Stande mit meinem Herzen zu
kämpfen hatte,—und ich war doch ein
ganz anderer Kerl als du, mit deiner
feinen Haut und deinen weichen Händer.

Rocco:
Bravo! very fine! If I were to tell you
how I had to struggle with my heart in
my early days, I should make you weep;
and I was quite a different fellow from
you, with your soft skin and delicate
hands.

Trio: Rocco, Marzelline, Leonore

Rocco:
Gut, Söhnchen, gut!
Hab' immer Muth,
Dann wird dir's auch gelingen
Das Herz wird hart
Durch Gegenwart
Bei fürchterlichen Dingen.

Rocco:
Courage! Be firm!
Protect your vigor
Proof you will see very soon.
In time your gentle heart will harden:
it changes
with all things down below.

Leonore:
Ich habe Muth
Mit kaltem Blut
Will ich hinab mich wagen.
Für hohen Lohn
Kann Liebe schon
Auch hohe Leiden tragen.

Leonore:
I have no fear
and would dare go below with you
to see where he languishes.
Love, when obeyed,
can bear the highest reward,
and the keenest anguish.

Marzelline:
Dein gutes Herz
Wird manchen schmerz
In diesen Gruften leiden;
Dann kehrt zuruck
Der Liebe Glück,
Und unnennbare Freuden.

Marzelline:
Your kindly heart
will shrink
within those dark recesses.
Then, after the gloom
true love will come
to cheer and bless your heart.

Rocco:
Du wirst dein Glück ganz sicher bau'n.

Rocco:
Your happiness will be secure.

Leonore:
Ich hab' auf Gott und Recht Vertrau'n

Leonore:
I trust heaven, my right place.

Marzelline:
Du darfst mir auch ins Auge schau'n;
Der Liebe Macht ist auch nicht klein.

Marzelline:
Yes, fate will propitiously smile,
and love will sustain your just actions.

Alle drei:
Ja, ja, wir werden glücklich seyn.

All:
Yes, yes, love will sustain me.

Rocco:
Der Gouverneur soll heut' erlauben,
Das du mit mir die Arbeit theilst.

Rocco:
The Governor should allow you to work
with me today.

Leonore:
Du wirst mir alle Ruhe rauben,
Wenn du bis morgen nur verweilst.

Leonore:
Ah! Heaven will assist the just —
but no longer delay me.

Marzelline:
Ja, guter Vater, bitt' ihn heute,
In Kurzem sind wir dann ein Paar.

Marzelline:
Yes, good father, plead with the Governor
to-day, so we may soon be united.

Rocco:
Ich bin ja bald des Grabes beute.

Rocco:
I shall soon go down to my grave.

Leonore:
Wie lang bin ich des Kummers Beute.

Leonore:
How long have I endured this agony?

Rocco:
Ich brauche Hülf', es ist ja wahr.

Rocco:
Yes, I truly need assistance.

Leonore:
Du, Hoffnung, reichst mir Labung dar.

Leonore:
Providence has sent me a gleam of hope.

Marzelline:
Ach, lieber Vater, was fällt Euch ein?
Lang' Freund und Rather müsst Ihr uns
seyn.

Marzelline:
Ah, dear father, do not despair.
You will, I hope, have a long life
to comfort and to protect.

Rocco:
Nur auf der huth,
Dann geht es gut,
Gestillt wird Euer Sehnen.

Rocco:
Be on your guard,
then all will go well,
and the wishes of all will be satisfied

Marzelline:
O, habe Muth,
O, welche Gluth!
O, welch' ein tiefes Sehnen.

Marzelline:
Oh yes, have courage.
What anxiety he now displays —
What yearning!

Leonore:
Ihr seyd so gut,
Ihr macht mir Muth,
Gestillt wird bald mein Sehnen.

Leonore:
You are both so kind.
You encourage my hope. I trust that
my wish will soon be satisfied.

Rocco:
Gebt Euch die Hand,
Und schliesst das Band

Rocco:
Now join hands, and sanctify this tender
knot with tears of joy.

Leonore:
Ich gab die Hand
Zum süssen Band.

Leonore:
I have given my sacred pledge.
Ah! what bitter tears it has cost me.

Marzelline:
Ein festes Band
Mit Herz und Hand

Marzelline:
A lasting tie, with hand and heart.
Oh! sweet and welcome tears.

Rocco:
In süssen Freudenthränen.

Rocco:
Sweet tears of joy.

Leonore:
Es kostet bittre Thränen.

Leonore:
It costs bitter tears

Marzelline:
O, süsse, süsse Thränen.

Marzelline: .
Oh! sweet, sweet tears.

Rocco:
Aber nun ist es auch Zeit, dass ich dem
Gouverneur die Briefschaften überbringe.
Ah! Er kommt selbst hierher.

Gieb sie, Fidelio, und dann entfernt euch!

Rocco:
It's time for me to deliver these letters
and dispatches to the Governor.
Ah! Here he comes!
(to Leonore)
Fidelio, give them to him, and then be off!

Leonore hands Rocco the tin box, and then exits to the house with
Marzelline.Officers and soldiers march, followed by Pizarro.

Pizarro:
Drei Mann Wache auf den Wall, sechs
Mann Tag und Nacht an der Zugbrücke,
eben so viel gegen den Garten zu; und
Jedermann, der sich dem Graben nähert,
werde sogleich vor mich gebracht.
Rokko, ist etwas Neues vorgefallen?

Pizarro: *(to the Officer)*
Three guards at the wall and on the drawbridge. Six men day and night, and six in the
garden; and anyone approaching the moat,
let him be brought before me immediately.
(to Rocco)
Has anything new happened?

Rocco:
Nein, Herr!

Rocco:
No, sir!

Pizarro:
Wo sind die Despeschen?

Pizarro:
Where are the dispatches?

Rocco:
Hier sind sie.

Rocco:
Here they are.
(He removes the letters from the tin box)

Pizarro:
Immer Emptehlungen und Vorwürfe.
Wenn ich auf Alles das achten wollte,
würde ich nie damit fertig werden.
Was seh' ich? Mich dünkt, ich kenne
diese Schrift. Lass sehen.

"Iche gebe Ihnen Nachricht, dass der
Minister in Erfahrung gebracht hat, dass
die Staats-Gefängnisse denen Sie
vorstehen, mehrere Opfer willkührlicher
Gewalt enthalten. Er reis't morgen ab,
um Sie mit einer Untersuchung zu
überiaschen. Seyn Sie auf Ihrer Huth,
und suchen Sie sich sicher zu stellen."

Gott! Wenn er entdeckte, dass ich diesen
Florestan in Ketten liegen habe, den er
längst todt glaubt, ihn, der so oft meine
Rache reizte, wenn er mich vor ihm
enthüllen und mir seine Gunst entziehen
würde! Doch es giebt ein Mittel!
Eine kühne that kann alle Besorgnisse
zerstreuen!

Aria: Pizarro and Soldiers
Ha! Welch' ein Augenblick!
Die Rache werd' ich kühlen,
Dich rufet dein Geschick!
In seinem Herzen wühlen,
O Wonne, grosses Glück!
Schon war ich nah' im Staube,
Dem lauten Spott zum Raube,
Dahin gestreckt zu sein.
Nun ist es mir geworden,
Den Mörder selbst zu morden.
In seiner letzten Stunde,
Den Stahl in seiner Wunde,
Ihm noch ins Ohr zu schrei'n:
Triumph! Der Sieg ist mein!

Soldaten:
Er spricht von Tod und Wunde—
nun fort auf unsre Runde!
Wie wichtig muss es sein
Rache werd'ich kühlen!
Nun, nun ist es mir gewordem
Mörder seibst zu morden!

Pizarro: *(looking through the papers)*
More recommendations! More
reproaches! If I attended to all of those
things, I would never have rest. Ah! what
do I see? I think I know this hand—let's
see.
(Pizarro reads the letter)
"I must inform you
that the Minister has learned that the
state prisons over which you preside
contain several victims who have been
arbitrarily confined. He sets out
tomorrow to surprise you with an
investigation. Be on your guard,
and protect yourself."

Heavens! If he should discover that I
have Florestan lying here in chains.
Florestan, who so often aroused my
vengeance, and the man he thought dead
long ago! I must not be unmasked and
lose the Governor's favor. But there is
one bold deed that can dissipate all my
fears and anxieties!

Pizarro:
Ah, the time has arrived!
I'll take revenge on him,
Your fate is calling you!
I shall probe his heart,
Oh joy, what great delight!
I almost was in the dust,
at the sneering scoffer's mercy,
knocked miserably down.
But my chance has come
to be the murderer's slayer;
in his final hour,
this steel, deep in his wound,
shall shout into his ears.
Triumph! Victory is mine!

Soldiers:
He speaks of death and wounds!
Let's go on our rounds!
How important it must be!
He speaks of death and wounds!
Look out, when on your rounds!
How important it must be!

Pizarro:
Ich darf keinen Augenblick säumen, alle
Anstalten zu meinem Vorhaben au
treffen. Heute soll der Minister
ankommen. Nur die grösste Vorsicht une
Eile Können mich retten.

Hauptmann! Besteigen Sie mit einem
Trompeter den Thurm; sehen Sie mit der
grössten Achtsamkeit auf die Strasse von
Sevilla; sobald Sie einen Wagen, von
Reitern umgeben, gewahr werden, geben
Sie augenblicklich ein Zeichen. Verstehen
Sie? augenblicklich! Ich erwarte die
grösste Pünktlichkeit; Sie haften mir mit
Ihrem Kopfe dafür. Fort auf Eure Posten!

Offizier:
Gewehr auf! Marsch!

Pizarro:
He!

Rocco:
Herr!

Pizarro:
Ich muss ihn zu gewinnen suchen. Ohne
seine Hilfe kann ich es nicht ausführen.
Komm näher!

Duet: Pizarro, Rocco
Pizarro:
Jetzt, Alter, jetzt hat es Eile!
Dir wird ein Glück zuteile,
Du wirst ein reicher Mann;
Das geb ich nur daran.

Rocco:
So sagt doch nur in Eile,
Womit ich dienen kann.

Pizarro:
Du bist von kaltem Blute,
Von unverzagtem Mute
Durch langen Dienst geworden.

Pizarro:
I don't not a moment to waste in getting
everything ready for my scheme.
The Minister is to arrive today.
Only the utmost precaution and haste can
save us!

Captain, take the trumpeter with you and
ascend the tower. Keep a vigil along the
road to Seville. As soon as you see a
carriage with noble escort, let the bugler
give an instant signal.
Away! And mind your orders! Do you
understand me? Neglect them, and your
head shall be the forfeit.
Away! Everyone to his post.

Officer:
Shoulder arms! Forward march!

Pizarro: *(to Rocco)*
Hey!

Rocco:
Sir!

Pizarro:
I must try to win him over. Without his
help I cannot carry it out!
Come over here!

Pizarro: *(showing him a purse)*
Take this, old man. Henceforth fortune
shall be yours;
if you yield your services to me,
you shall be a rich man.

Rocco:
Speak on. Quickly tell me in what way I
can serve you?

Pizarro:
I know your zeal and coolness,
and what I shall now reveal to you,
I think I can trust you to confide.

Rocco:
Was soll ich? Redet! Redet!

Pizarro:
Morden!

Rocco:
Wie?

Pizarro:
Höre mich nur an!
Du bebst? Bist du ein Mann?
Wir dürfen gar nicht säumen;
Dem Staate liegt daran,
Den bösen Untertan
Schnell aus dem Weg zu räumen.

Rocco:
O Herr!

Pizarro:
Du stehst noch an?
Er darf nicht länger leben,
Sonst ist's um mich geschehn.
Pizarro sollte beben?
Du fällst - ich werde stehn.

Rocco:
Die Glieder fühl' ich beben,
Wie könnt ich das bestehn?
Ich nehm' ihm nicht das Leben,
Mag, was da will, geschehen?

Nein Herr, das Leben nehmen,
Das ist nicht meine Pflicht.

Pizarro:
Ich will micht selbst bequemen,
Wenn dir's an Muth gebricht.
Nur eile, rash und munter
Zu jenem Mann hinunter
Du weisst

Rocco:
Der kaum mehr lebt,
Und wie ein Schatten schwebet.

Rocco:
Speak! What shall I do?

Pizarro:
Murder!

Rocco: *(terrified)*
What?

Pizarro:
Simply listen—but do not tremble!
Are you trembling? Are you a man?
We must delay this no longer
or I shall be undone. The state is
concerned with that troublesome inmate
of yours. He must quickly be rid of.

Rocco:
Oh Sir!

Pizarro: *(to himself)*
You still hesitate! He must live no longer,
or I shall be undone!
Should Pizarro live in fear?
See how it is, you falter;
but I will stand my ground.

Rocco:
I feel my limbs quake under me.
How should I undertake this?
If I do not take his life,
what will happen?

No, Sir, to take a life
is not my duty.

Pizarro:
I do not want to be comfortable myself,
if that deprives you of courage.
Just rush, be rash and cheerful
and go down to that man.
You understand. Let happen what may.

Rocco: *(Offering to return the purse)*
He is scarcely alive
and seems like a mere shadow.

Pizarro:
Zu dem, zu dem hinab—
Ich wart' in kleiner Ferne,
Du gräbst in der Cisterne
Sehr schnell für ihn ein Grab.

Pizarro: *(fiercely).*
Go down, I say, go down to him.
I will wait a short distance away.
Dig a grave for him in the cistern
of the prison, without delay.

Rocco:
Und denn?

Rocco:
And then?

Pizarro:
Du giebst ein Zeichen,
Dann werd ich ruhig sein.
Schnell in der Kerker schleichen:
Ein Stoss—und er verstummt.

Pizarro:
You must give me a signal,
and then I'll steal away, in disguise,
and go directly into the dungeon.
One blow—and he is finished.

Rocco:
Verhungernd in den Ketten,
Ertrug er lange Pein
Ihn tödten, heisst ihn retten.
Der dolch wird ihn befrein.

Rocco:
Half famished, and in chains,
he has long endured the severest misery.
To rid him of life would be to release him
from his agony.

Pizarro:
Dann werd ich ruhig seyn.

Pizarro:
Then I shall be at peace.

Aria: Leonore

Abscheulicher! Wo eilst du hin?
Was hast du vor in wildem Grimme?
Des Mitleids Ruf,
der Menschheit Stimme,
Rührt nichts mehr deinen Tigersinn?
Doch toben auch wie Meereswogen
Dir in der Seele Zorn und Wut,
So leuchtet mir ein Farbenbogen,
Der hell auf dunklen Wolken ruht:
Der blickt so still,
so friedlich nieder,
Der spiegelt alte Zeiten wieder,
Und neu besänftigt wallt mein Blut.

You monster! Where will you go?
What cruel fury have you planned?
The call of pity,
or the voice of mankind,
will nothing move your tiger's wrath?
Like the surge of ocean's waves,
ire and anger in your heart,
a rainbow on my path still shines,
which brightly rests on somber clouds:
It looks so calm
and peacefully at me,
reminding me of happier days
and thus soothe my troubled heart.

Komm, Hoffnung, lass den letzten Stern
Der Müden nicht erbleichen!
Erhell mein Ziel, sei's noch so fern,
Die Liebe wird's erreichen.
Ich folg' dem innern Triebe,
Ich wanke nicht,
Mich stärkt die Pflicht
Der treuen Gattenliebe!

Come, hope, let not the last bright star
of my anguish be obscured!
Light up my goal, however far,
I shall reach, through love.
I follow my inner calling,
and shall not waver.
I derive strength
from faithfulness and love!

O du, für den ich alles trug,
Könnt' ich zur Stelle dringen,
Wo Bosheit dich in Fesseln schlug,
Und süssen Trost dir bringen!
Ich folg' dem innern Triebe,
Ich wanke nicht,
Mich stärkt die Pflicht
Der treuen Gattenliebe!

Oh you, for whom I bore so much,
if I could penetrate
where malice has imprisoned you,
and bring you sweet comfort!
I follow my inner calling,
and shall not waver.
I derive strength
from faithfulness and love.

Marzelline and Jaquino enter from the house.

Jaquino:
Aber Marzelline—

Jaquino:
But, Marzelline!

Marzelline:
Kein Wort, keine Sylbe! Ich will nichts
mehr von deinen albernen Liebeseufzern
hören, und dabei bleibts.

Marzelline: .
Not a word—be quiet! I do not wish to
hear another word of your silly sighing
and nonsense.

Jaquino:
Wer das gesagt hätte, als ich mir
vornahm, mich recht ordentlich in dich zu
verlieben: da war ich der gute, der liebe
Jaquino! aber dieser Fidelio—

Jaquino:
Who would have said, that when I
decided to fall in love with you, then I
was your choice, dear Jaquino, but now
it is Fidelio.

Marzelline:
Ich läugne nicht, ich war dir gut; aber
sieh—ich bin offenherzig—das war keine
Liebe. Fidelio zieht mich weit mehr an;
zwischen ihm und mir find' ich eine viel
grössere Uebereinstimmung.

Marzelline:
Very true. I liked you at first, or I fancied
so—I may as well be frank and open
with you. But, since Fidelio has been
among us, my mind has changed: I have
much more feeling for him.

Jaquino:
Eine Uebereinstimmung mit einem
solchen hergelaufenen Jungen, der, Gott
weiss woher kommt; den der Vater aus
blossem Mitleid am Thore dort
aufgenommen hat, der—der—

Jaquino:
What! For a young vagabond
who comes—God knows from where;
and who your father
housed in charity;
who—who—

Marzelline:
Der arm und verlassen ist, und den ich
dennoch heirathen werde.

Marzelline: *(angrily)*
Who is poor and deserted, and shall be
my spouse, notwithstanding.

Jaquino:
Glaubst du, dass ich das leiden werde?
He! dass es ja nicht in meiner Gegenwart
geschieht; ich möchte Euch einen
gewaltigen Streich spielen.

Jaquino:
And do you imagine that I will suffer it?
No, no, believe me.
If ever I catch you together, you shall see
what I will do.

Rocco and Leonore enter.

Rocco:
Was habt ihr Beide denn wieder zu zanken?

Rocco:
What! Are you two quarrelling again?

Marzelline:
Ach, Vater, er verfolgt mich immer!

Marzelline:
Ah, father, he is always teasing me!

Rocco:
Warum denn?

Rocco:
About what?

Marzelline:
Er will, dass ich ihn lieben, dass ich ihn heirathen soll?

Marzelline: *(rushing to Leonora)*
He wishes me to love him—to marry him!

Jaquino:
Ja, ja, sie soll mich lieben, sie soll mich wenigstens heirathen, und ich—

Jaquino:
Yes, sir, and if she will not love me, she shall at least marry me; and I—

Rocco:
Stille! Ich werde eine einzige gute Tochter haben, werde sie so gut gepflegt mit so viel Mühe bis in ihr sechzehntes Jahr erzogen haben, und das Alles für den Herrn da? Nein, Jaquino, mich beschäftigen jetzt andere klügere Dinge.

Rocco:
Hold your tongue! For such a gentleman, I have brought up my only daughter with parental care, that increases with years, till she has seen her sixteenth summer, Ha! ha! No, Jaquino. But weighty matters now engage my mind.

Marzelline:.
Ich verstehe, Vater, Fidelio.

Marzelline:
I understand, dear father, Fidelio!

Leonore:
Brechen wir davon ab. Rokko, ich ersuchte Euch schon einigemal, die armen Gefangenen die hier über der Erde wohnen, in unsern Festungsgarten zu lassen. Ihr verspracht und verschobt es immer. Heute ist das Wetter so schön. Der Gouverneur kommt um diese Zeit nicht hieher.

Leonore:
Enough of this. Rocco, often I have begged of you to allow the poor prisoners, immured in this dismal cell, to come and breathe the pure air of this garden. Though often promised, you have never yet done it. Today the weather is so beautiful! The Governor never comes at this time of day.

Marzelline:
O ja, ich bitte mit ihm!

Marzelline:
Oh yes, I too ask it!

Rocco:
Kinder,—ohne Erlaubniss des Gouverneurs?

Rocco:
Without permission of the Governor? My dear children—

Marzelline:
Aber er sprach so lange mit Euch?
Vielleicht sollt Ihr ihm einen Gefallen thun,
und dann wird er's so genau nicht nehmen.

Marzelline:
But he was talking with you so long:
perhaps he was asking a favor? In that
case, he could not be very particular.

Rocco:
Einen Gefallen? Du hast Recht,
Marzelline! Auf diese Gefahr kann ich's
wagen. Wohl denn. Jaquino und Fidelio
öffnet die leichtern Gefängnisse. Ich aber
gehe zu Pizarro und halte ihn auf, indem
ich für dein Bestes rede.

Rocco:
A favor? Well guessed, Marzelline.
I think I may venture.
It's Jaquino and Fidelio, you may open
the door.
I'll converse with Pizarro on your behalf.
Keep them busy.

Marzelline:
So recht, Vater!

Marzelline:
Oh, blessings on you, father dear!

Rocco departs. Leonore and Jaquino open the Prison doors, then withdraw.
Marzelline stands in the background and observes the Prisoners with interest
as they gradually enter the garden.

Chor der Gegangenen:
O welche Lust, in freier Luft
Den Atem leicht zu heben!
Nur hier, nur hier ist Leben!
Der Kerker eine Gruft.

Prisoners' Chorus:
Oh what joy, in the open air,
free to breathe again!
Up here life is lonely!
The dungeon is a grave.

Erster Gefangener:
Wir wollen mit Vertrauen
Auf Gottes Hilfe bauen!
Die Hoffnung flüstert sanft mir zu:
Wir werden frei, wir finden Ruh

First Prisoner:
With all our faith
we shall trust in God!
Hope whispers softly in my ears!
We shall be free, we shall find peace.

Alle Anderen:
O Himmel! Rettung! Welch ein Glück!
O Freiheit! Kehrst du zurück?

All Others:
Oh Heaven! Salvation! Happiness!
Oh Freedom! Will you be given to us?

Zweiter Gefangener:
Sprecht leise! Haltet euch zurück!
Wir sind belauscht mit Ohr und Blick.

Second Prisoner:
Speak softly! Be on your guard!
We are watched with eye and ear.

Alle:
Sprecht leise! Haltet euch zurück!
Wir sind belauscht mit Ohr und Blick. -
O welche Lust, in freier Luft
Den Atem leicht zu heben!
Nur hier, nur hier ist Leben.

All:
Speak softly! Be on your guard!
We are watched with eye and ear.
Oh what joy, in the open air,
free to breathe again!
Up here life is lonely.

Leonore and Rocco

Leonore:
Nun sprecht, wie ging's?

Rocco:
Recht gut, recht gut!
Zusammen rafft ich meinen Mut
Und trug ihm alles vor;
Und sollst du's glauben,
Was er zur Antwort mir gab?
Die Heirat und dass du mir hilfst, will er erlauben;
Noch heute führ' ich in den Kerker dich hinab.

Leonore:
Noch heute! Noch heute!
O welch ein Glück! O welche Wonne!

Rocco:
Ich sehe deine Freude;
Nur noch ein Augenblick.
Dann gehen wir schon beide...

Leonore:
Wohin?

Rocco
Zu jenem Mann hinab,
Dem ich seit vielen Wochen
Stets weniger zu essen gab.

Leonore:
Ha! Wird er losgesprochen?

Rocco:
O nein!

Leonore:
So sprich!

Rocco:
O nein, O nein!
Wir müssen ihn, doch wie? Befrein!
Denn nach Pizarros Wille
Muss er in aller Stille
Von uns begraben sein!

Leonore:
How did it go?

Rocco:
Quite well, quite well!
I gathered all my courage
and told him everything.
And would you believe
what he replied to me?
He will permit your marriage
and as long as you help me.
Today, I shall lead you
down into the dungeon.

Leonore:
Today! Today!
What happiness, what great joy!

Rocco:
I can see your joy.
It'll only be for one moment,
and We shall go together...

Leonore:
Where?

Rocco:
To that man down below,
to whom I gave
less and less to eat, for weeks.

Leonore:
Ah! Will he be released?

Rocco:
Oh no!

Leonore:
Tell me!

Rocco:
Oh no, oh, no!
We have to, how shall I say, free him.
We must do it within one hour.
No one else may know
that we both buried him!

Leonore:
So ist er tot?

Rocco:
Noch nicht, noch nicht.

Leonore:
Icht?

Rocco:
Nein guter Junge, zittre nicht,
Zum Morden dingt sich Rocco nicht.
Der Gouverneur kommt selbst hinab,
Wir beide graben nur das Grab.

Leonore:
Vielleicht das Grab des Gatten graben,
Was kann fürchterlicher sein?

Rocco:
Ich darf ihn nicht mit Speise laben,
Ihm wird im Grabe besser sein.
Wir müssen gleich zu Werke schreiten,
Du musst mir helfen, mich begleiten;
Hart ist des Kerkermeisters Brot.

Leonore:
Ich folge dir, wär's in den Tod.

Rocco:
In der zerfallenen Zisterne
Bereiten wir die Grube leicht.
Ich tu es, glaube mir, nicht gerne;
Auch dir ist schaurig, wie mich deucht?

Leonore:
Ich bin es nur noch nicht gewohnt.

Rocco:
Ich hätte gerne dich verschont,
Doch wird es mir allein zu schwer,
Und gar so streng ist unser Herr.

Leonore:
O welch ein Schmerz!

Rocco:
Mir scheint, er weine. Nein, du bleibst
hier - ich geh alleine, Ich geh allein.

Leonore:
So he is to die?

Rocco:
Not yet, not yet.

Leonore:
To kill him, is this your duty?

Rocco:
No, my dear boy, don't be afraid;
Rocco cannot be hired for murder.
The governor himself comes,
we two, only we dig his grave.

Leonore:
To dig perhaps a husband's grave;
is there anything more cruel?

Rocco:
I'm not allowed to give him food,
The grave will be relief for him.
We must go to work at once.
You must come and assist me;
the jailer's life is a hard one.

Leonore:
I follow you, as if it were to my death.

Rocco:
We can easily dig the grave in the
crumbling cistern.
Believe me, I am loathe to do it;
You too, it seems, are shuddering.

Leonore:
I only am not used to it.

Rocco:
I wished I could have spared you this.
It gets to be too much even for me alone,
and our master is so severe.

Leonore:
Oh, what great pain!

Rocco:
I think he's crying. No, you stay here. I'll
go there alone, I'll go alone.

Leonore:
O nein, O nein!
Ich muss ihn sehn; den Armen sehen,
Und müsst ich selbst zugrunde gehen.

Rocco, Leonore:
O säumen wir nun länger nicht,
Wir folgen unsrer strengen Pflicht.

Quintet, Chorus:
Marcelline:
Ach, Vater, Vater, eilt!

Rocco:
Was hast du denn?

Jaquino:
Nicht länger weilt!

Rocco:
Was ist geschehn?

Marzelline:
Es folget mir Pizarro nach!
Er drohet dir.

Rocco:
Gemach! Gemach!

Leonore:
So eilet fort!

Rocco:
Nur noch dies Wort:
Sprich, weiss er schon?

Jaquino:
Ja, er weiss es schon.

Marzelline:
Der Offizier sagt ihm, was wir
Jetzt den Gefangenen gewähren.

Rocco:
Lasst alle schnell zurücke kehren.

Marzelline:
Ihr wisst ja, wie er tobet,
Und kennet seine Wut.

Leonore:
Oh no, oh no!
I must see him; see the poor man,
even if I have to perish.

Rocco, Leonore:
So let's no longer hesitate.
We have to do our cruel work.

Marcelline:
Quick, Father, quick!

Rocco:
What is it now?

Jaquino:
No longer wait!

Rocco:
What's happened now?

Marzelline:
Pizarro is following me!
He's threatening you.

Rocco:
Keep calm, keep calm!

Leonore:
Hurry along!

Rocco:
Just tell me this:
Does he know about all of this?

Jaquino:
Yes, he knows it all.

Marzelline:
The officer told him what we
allowed the prisoners to do.

Rocco:
Let all of them return quickly.

Marzelline:
We've seen him in rage before,
and we know his anger well.

Leonore:
Wie mir's im Innem tobet!
Empöret ist mein Blut.

Leonore:
My heart is tossing about,
and my blood is in a rage.

Rocco:
Mein Herz hat mich gelobet,
Wie mir's im Innem tobet!

Rocco:
My heart tosses inside of me.
May the tyrant rage.

Pizarro:
Verwegner Alter! Welche Rechte
Legst du dir frevelnd selber bei?
Und ziemt es dem gedungnen Knechte,
Zu geben die Gefangnen frei?

Pizarro:
Insolent old man! By what right
have you assumed such frivolous
behavior? Does it befit a hired servant
to give the prisoners freedom?

Rocco:
O Herr!

Rocco:
Oh Sir!

Pizarro:
Wohlan!

Pizarro:
Speak up!

Rocco:
Des Frühlings Kommen,
Das heitre warme Sonnenlicht,
Dann: habt Ihr wohl in acht genommen,
Was sonst zu meinem Vorteil spricht?
Des Königs Namensfest ist heute,
Das feiern wir auf solche Art.
Der unten stirbt - doch lasst die andern
Jetzt fröhlich hin und wieder wandern;
Für jenen sei der Zorn gespart.

Rocco:
The spring arrived,
and the sun is bright and warm.
And: Have you ever thought that
it might acquit me of my guilt?
His Majesty's birthday is today.
We celebrate it in this way.
The one below dies, but let the others
walk gaily to and fro;
spare all of your hatred for him.

Pizarro:
So eile, ihm sein Grab zu graben,
Hier will ich stille Ruhe haben.
Schliess' die Gefangnen wieder ein,
Mögst du nie mehr verwegen sein!

Pizarro:
So hurry up and dig his grave.
Up here I will have strict peace.
Lock the prisoners up again,
and may you never again be insolent!

Die Gegangenen:
Leb' wohl, du warmes Sonnenlicht,
Schnell schwindest du uns wieder;
Schon sinkt die Nacht hernieder,
Aus der so bald kein Morgen bricht.

The Prisoners:
Farewell, warm sunshine,
we must leave you too quickly.
Already night is falling,
from which no tomorrow dawns so soon.

Marzelline:
Wie eilten sie zum Sonnenlicht
Und scheiden traurig wieder.
Die andern murmeln nieder:
Hier wohnt die Lust, die Freude nicht.

Marzelline:
How gaily did they greet the sun,
and now they part so sadly.
The others whisper to themselves:
this is no place for joy and pleasure.

Leonore:
Ihr hört das Wort, drum zögert nicht,
Kehrt in den Kerker wieder.
Angst rinnt durch meine Glieder.
Ereilt den Frevler kein Gericht?

Leonore:
You heard the word, don't hesitate:
return into your prison cells now.
Anxiety makes me tremble.
Is there no justice for the wicked?

Jaquino:
Ihr hört das Wort, drum zögert nicht,
Kehrt in den Kerker wieder.
Sie sinnen auf und nieder!
Könnt ich verstehn, was jeder spricht!

Jaquino:
You heard the word, don't hesitate,
Return into your prison cells now.
They whisper to each other.
I cannot hear what they all are saying.

Pizarro:
Nun, Rocco, zögre länger nicht,
Steig' in den Kerker nieder.
Nicht eher kehrst du wieder,
Bis ich vollzogen das Gericht.

Pizarro:
Now Rocco, no longer hesitate,
and descend down to the dungeon.
No sooner you will return,
I will have passed judgement on him.

Rocco:
Nein, Herr, ich zögre länger nicht,
Ich steige eilend nieder.
Mir beben meine Glieder;
O unglückselig harte Pflicht!

Rocco:
No, Sir, I shall not hesitate.
I'll hurriedly go down.
I am trembling all over,
oh dreadful, cruel duty!

END of ACT I

Act II — Music Highlight Index

Aria: Florestan (P 73)
Gott! welch ein Dunkel hier!

Duet: Leonore, Rocco (P 73)
Wie kalt ist es in diesem unterirdischen Gewölbe.

Duet: Leonore, Rocco (P 74)
Nur hurtig fort, nur frisch gegraben

Trio: Florestan, Rocco, Leonore (P 78)
Euch werde Lohn in bessern Welten

Quartet: Leonore, Rocco, Florestan, Pizarro (P 80)
Er sterbe!

Quartet: Leonore, Florestan (P 82)
Es schlägt der Rache Stunde.

Duet: Leonore, Florestan (P 83)
O namenlose Freude!

Alle: (P 84)
Heil sei dem Tag, Heil sei der Stunde

Quintet: Leonore (P 86)
O Gott! Welch ein Augenblick!

Act II
a dark, subterranean dungeon

Aria: Florestan

Gott! welch ein Dunkel hier!
O grauenvolle Stille! Oed ist es um mich
her. Nichts lebet ausser mir. O schwere
Prüfung! doch gerecht ist Gottes Wille,
Ich murre nicht, das Maass der Leiden
steht bei dir.

In des Lehens Frühlingstagen, ist das
Glück von mir gefloh'n. Wahrheit wagt
ich kühn zu sagen, und die Ketten sind
mein Lohn. Willig duld' ich alle
Schmerzen, Ende schmählich meine
Bahn; Süsser Trost in meinem Herzen:
Meine Pflicht hab' ich gethan.

Und spür' ich nicht linde, sanft
säuselnde Luft? und ist nicht mein Grab
mir erhellet? Ich seh', wie ein Engel im
rosigen Duft sich tröstend zur Seite mir
stellet, – ein Engel, Leonoren, der Gattin
so gleich, der führt mich zur Freiheit in's
himmlische Reich.

Florestan:

God! What dense darkness dense!
What horrid stillness! Here in this dark
tomb, nothing is known but my deep
anguish! Oh, most cruel torture!
Oh, Heavenly Providence, how much
longer will my misery last!

In the bright morning of life, alas, my
liberty, was lost: These chains are the
reward for speaking the truth.
But what avails my lamentations?
My condition is my condition:
The only solace for my torment rests on
my conscious innocence.

And I do not feel soft breezes and gently
whispering in the air? And isn't my grave
illuminated to me? I see an angel in the
rosy perfume being comforted to my
side. An angel, Leonore, my adored wife,
who leads me to freedom in the heavenly
kingdom.

Rocco and Leonore descend ino the dungeon, each carrying a pitcher and implements for digging.

Duet: Leonore, Rocco:

Wie kalt ist es in diesem unterirdischen
Gewölbe.

Leonore:

Oh, how freezing it is in this dismal
vault!

Rocco:

Das ist natürlich! Es ist ja so tief.

Rocco:

Natural enough for a place so subterranean.

Leonore:

Ich glaubte schon, wir würden den
Eingang nicht finden.

Leonore:

I thought we would never find the
entrance.

Rocco:

Still! da ist der Gefangene.

Rocco:

Quiet! The prisoner is there.

Leonore:

Er scheint ganz ohne Bewegung.

Leonore:

What a state—unconscious, motionless!

Rocco:

Vielleicht ist er todt!

Rocco:

Perhaps he is dead!

Leonore:
Ihr meiut es?

Leonore:
Do you think so?

Rocco:
Nein, nein, er schläft nur. Das müssen
wir benützen und gleich ans Werk gehen;
wir haben keine Zeit zu verlieren.

Rocco:
No, no; he only sleeps. The moment is
propitious. Give me your hand. Let's get
to work—we have no time to lose.

Leonore: .
Est ist unmöglich, seine Züge zu unterscheiden;
Gott stehe mir bei, wenn er es ist!

Leonore: *(aside)*
It is impossible to distinguish his
features: If it is him, oh God, help me.

Rocco:
Hier unter diesen Trümmern ist eine
Cisterne von der ich dir gesagt habe. Wir
brauchen nicht viel Zeit um an die
Oeffnung zu kommen. Gieb mir eine
Haue, und du stelle dich hierher. Du
zitterst—fürchtest du dich?

Rocco:
Here, under this rubbish, is the cistern of
which I have spoken. It will not take us
long to reach the opening.
Give me the axe, and stand over there.
You're trembling—what are you afraid
of?

Leonore:
O nein, es ist nur so kalt.

Leonore:
Oh, no! only it is so cold!

Rocco:
So mach' fort, beim Arbeiten wird dir
schon warm werden.

Rocco:
Go on, you'll keep warm through
working.

Rocco and Leonore descend the stairs, with a pitcher and digging implements.

Duet: Leonore, Rocco:
Nur hurtig fort, nur frisch gegraben,
Es währt nicht lang', er kommt herein.

Rocco:
Only hurry up before he comes in.
A fresh dig doesn't last too long.

Leonore:
Ihr sollt ja nicht zu klagen haben,
Ihr sollt gewiss zufrieden sein.

Leonore:
You should not be complaining.
You should certainly be satisfied.

Rocco:
Komm, hilf doch diesen Stein mir
heben.Hab' acht! Hab' acht! Er hat Gewicht!

Rocco:
Come, help me lift this stone.
Be careful! Be careful! It's quite heavy!

Leonore:
Ich helfe schon - sorgt Euch nicht; Ich
will mir alle Mühe geben.

Leonore:
I'll help you - do not worry;
I want to give you all me efforts.

Rocco:
Ein wenig noch!

Rocco:
A little more!

Leonore:
Geduld!

Rocco:
Er weicht.

Leonore:
Nur etwas noch!
Lasst mich nur wieder Kräfte haben,
Wir werden bald zu Ende sein. Wer du
auch seist, ich will dich retten, Bei Gott!
Du sollst kein Opfer sein! Gewiss, ich
löse deine Ketten. Ich will, du Armer,
dich befrein.

Rocco:
Was zauderst du in deiner Pflicht?

Leonore:
Mein Vater, nein, ich zaudre nicht.
Ihr sollt ja nicht zu klagen haben, Lasst
mich nur wieder Kräfte haben. Denn mir
wird keine Arbeit schwer.

Er erwacht!

Rocco:.
Er erwacht, sagst du?

Leonore:
Ja, er hat eben den Kopf in die Höhe gehoben.

Rocco:
Ohne Zweifel wird er wieder tausend
Fragen an mich stellen. Ich muss allein
mit ihm reden. Nun bald hat er's
überstanden. Steig du, statt nieiner,
hinab, und räume noch so viel hinweg,
dass man die Cisterne öffnen kann.

Leonore:
Was in mir vorgeht, ist unaussprechlich!

Rocco:
Nun, Ihr habt wieder einige Augenblicke
geruht?

Leonora:
Patience!

Rocco:
It's giving way.

Leonore:
Only something else!
Let me just have my strength again.
It will be over soon. Whoever you are,
I want to save you, By God! You should
not be a victim! Certainly, I will loosen
your chains. I want you, poor thing, I
want to free you.

Rocco:
Why are you so zealous in your duty?

Leonore:
My father, no, I'm not hesitating.
You should not have to complain. Let me
only have my strength again, because no
work is difficult for me.

He is waking!

Rocco:
He's awake, you say?

Leonore:
Yes, yes; he has just raised his head.

Rocco:
No doubt he will again ask me a
thousand questions. I must speak with
him alone. Well, it will soon be over for
him. You go down, and clear away the
earth, and open the cistern.

Leonore: *(trembling)*
Who could explain my fears!

Rocco: *(to Florestan)*
Well, friend, are you again losing your
cares in rest?

Florestan:
Geruht? Wie fände ich Ruhe?

Florestan:
Repose! Where can I find it?

Leonora:
Diese stimme! Wenn ich nur einen
Augenblick sein Gesicht sehen könnte

Leonora: *(to herself)*
That voice! If I could only see his face
for an instant!

Florestan:
Werdet Ihr immer bei meinen Klagen taub
seyn, grausamer Mann?

Florestan:
Cruel man! Will you always be deaf to
my lamentations?

At these words, Florestan turns towards Leonore, who recognizes him.

Leonore:
Gott! Er ist's!

Leonore:
Oh, God! It is him!

Rocco:
Was verlangt Ihr denn von mir? Ich
vollziehe die Befehle die man mir giebe;
das ist mein Amt, meine Pflicht.

Rocco:
What do you ask of me? The orders I
receive I execute: that is my province,
my duty.

Florestan:
Saget mir endlich einmal, wer ist der
Gouverneur dieses Getängnisses?

Florestan:
Tell me, at all events, the name of the
Governor of this loathsome prison?

Rocco:
Jetzt kann ich ihm ja ohne Gefahr genug
thun. Der Gouverneur dieses
Gefängnisses ist Don Pizarro.

Rocco: *(aside)*
There can be no harm in now telling him.
The Governor of this prison is Don
Pizarro.

Leonore:
O Barbar! deine Grausamkeit giebt mir
meine Kräfte wieder.

Leonore:
Oh, barbarian! Your cruelty restores my
inherent strength.

Florestan:
O schickt sobald als möglich nach Sevilla,
fragt nach Leonoren Florestan.

Florestan:
Oh! If it be possible, let a messenger go
to Seville, and there seek Leonore.

Leonore:.
Gott! Er ahnet nicht, dass sie jezt sein
Grab gräbt.

Leonore:
Little does he think, oh God, that she is
now digging his grave!

Florestan:.
Sagt ihr, dass ich hier in Ketten liege.

Florestan:
Tell her that I lie here in chains.

Rocco:
Es ist unmoglich, sag' ich Euch; ich
würde mich ins Verderben stürzen, ohne
Euch genützt zu haben.

Rocco:
It is not possible. I tell you; I would
plunge myself into ruin without helping
you.

Florestan:
Wenn ich denn verdammt binn, hier zu
verschmachten, O so lasst mich nicht so
langsam enden!

Florestan:
Well, if here I am to languish here,
let me not go so slowly and linger to my
end!

Leonore:
O Gott! wer kann dass ertragen?

Leonore:
Oh, God! who could endure this torture?

Florestan:
Aus Erbarmen, gebt mir nur einen
Tropfen Wasser—das ist ja so wenig!

Florestan:
Out of mercy, give me a drop of water, a
small favor for my parched lips!

Rocco:
Es geht mir wider meinen Willen zu Herzen.

Rocco:
He touches my heart, in spite of myself.

Leonore:
Er scheint ihn zu erweichen.

Leonore:
He seems to be easing up.

Florestan:
Du giebst mir keine Antwort.

Florestan:
You dost not answer me.

Rocco:
Ich kann Euch nicht verschaffen, was Ihr
verlangt. Alles was ich Euch anbieten
kann, ist ein Restchen Wein, das ich im
Kruge habe.

Rocco:
What you ask I cannot do.
All that I can offer him
is the little wine that I have remaining.

Leonore:.
Da ist er—da ist er.

Leonore:
There it is—there it is.

Florestan:
Wer ist das?

Florestan: *(staring at Leonore)*
Who is he?

Rocco:
Mein schliesser und in wenig Tagen mein
Eidam. Es ist freilich nur ein wenig.
Wein, aber icj gebe ih Euch gern. Du bist
ganz in Bewegung?

Rocco:
At present my assistant; but soon he will
be my son-in-law. There is little wine, I
see; but what there is you're welcome to.
(to Leonora)] How agitated you are?

Leonore:
We sollte es nicht sein? Ihn selbst,
Meister Rocco.

Leonora: *(extremely embarrassed)*
Who would not be so? You yourself,
Master Rocco.

Rocco:
Es ist wahe, der Mensch had si eine
Stimme.

Rocco:
True: the sounds of his voice are so
touching.

Leonore::
Ja wohl, sie dringt in die Tiefe, des
Herzens.

Leonore:
They are—they stab me, which goes to
the very depths of my heart.

Trio: Florestan, Rocco, Leonore:

Euch werde Lohn in bessern Welten,
Der Himmel hat euch mir geschickt.
O Dank! Ihr habt mich süss erquickt;
Ich kann die Wohltat, ich kann sie nicht
vergelten.

Florestan:
May reward be yours in better worlds.
You have been sent to me by God.
Oh thanks, you've sweetly refreshed me;
I cannot repay your kindness.

Rocco:
Ich lab' ihn gern, den armen Mann,
Es ist ja bald um ihn getan.

Rocco:
I gladly refresh the poor man.
It will soon be over for him.

Leonore:
Wie heftig pochet dieses
Es wogt in Freud' und scharfem Schmerz.

Leonore:
How furiously my heart throbs.
In joy it surges and stings in pain,

Florestan:
Bewegt seh' ich den Jüngling hier,
Und Rührung zeigt auch dieser Mann.
O Gott, du sendest Hoffnung mir,
Dass ich sie noch gewinnen kann.

Florestan:
I see this youth so deeply moved;
compassion also shows in this man.
Oh God, you've given me fresh hope.
May it become true in the end.

Leonore:
Die hehre, bange Stunde winkt,
Die Tod mir oder Rettung bringt.

Leonore:
The great and anxious hour nears,
which brings me salvation or death.

Rocco:
Ich tu, was meine Pflicht gebeut,
Doch hass' ich alle Grausamkeit.

Rocco:
I'm always bound by my duty,
but I also hate all cruelty.

Leonore:
Dies Stückchen Brot - ja, seit zwei Tagen
Trag' ich es immer schon bei mir.

Leonore:
This piece of bread - yes, I've carried it
around with me for two days.

Rocco:
Ich möchte gern, doch sag' ich dir,
Das hiesse wirklich zu viel wagen.

Rocco:
I've wanted to, but believe me,
this venture has been too much.

Leonore:
Ach! Ihr labtet gern den armen Mann.

Leonore:
You gladly inspired this poor man.

Rocco:
Das geht nicht an, das geht nicht an.

Rocco:
This cannot be, this cannot be.

Leonore:
Es ist ja bald um ihn getan.

Rocco:
So sei es - ja, so sei's - du kannst es
wagen.

Leonore:
Da, nimm das Brot - du armer Mann!

Florestan:
O Dank dir, Dank! - O Dank! O Dank!
Euch werde Lohn in bessern Welten,
Der Himmel hat euch mir geschickt.
O Dank! Ihr habt mich süss erquickt,
Ich kann die Wohltat nicht vergelten.

Leonore:
Der Himmel schicke Rettung dir,
Dann wird mir hoher Lohn gewährt.

Rocco:
Mich rührte oft dein Leiden hier,
Doch Hilfe war mir streng verwehrt.
Ich labt' ihn gern, den armen Mann,
Es ist ja bald um ihn getan.

Leonore:
O mehr, als ich ertragen kann!

Florestan:
O dass ich euch nicht lohnen kann!

Rocco:
Ist alles bereit? Ich gehe, das Signal zu
geben.

Leonore:
Mussich nicht dem Gefangenen die Eisen
abnehmen? Geh! Geh!

Pizarro:
Die muss ich mir noch heute beide vom
Halse schaffen, damit alles auf immer
verborgen bleibt.

Rocco:
Soll ich ihm die Ketten abnehmen?

Leonore:
It will soon be over for him.

Rocco:
So be it - yes, so be it - you may do it.

Leonore:
Here, take the bread - you poor, poor
man!

Florestan:
Oh thanks to you! Oh thanks! Oh thanks!
May reward be yours in better worlds.
You have been sent to me by God.
Oh thanks! You've sweetly renewed me.
I cannot repay your kindness.

Leonore:
May Heaven grant you salvation,
then a high reward will come to me.

Rocco:
Your suffering has often moved me,
But I've not been allowed to help.
I refreshed him gladly, the poor man,
It will soon be over for him.

Leonore:
Oh, this is more than I can bear!

Florestan:
Oh, that I cannot reward you!

Rocco:
Everything is ready. Fidelio, stay here, I
shall go to give the governor the signal.

Leonore:
Shouldn't I take off the prisoner's
chains? Now go!

Pizarro:
I must get rid of those two as soon as I
can, so that everything stays hidden
forever.

Rocco:
Shall I remove his chains?

Pizarro:
Nein, aber sschliesse ihn von dem Stein
los. Die Zeit ist dringend.

Quartet: Leonore, Rocco, Florestan,
Pizarro:
Er sterbe!
Doch er soll erst wissen,
Wer ihm sein stolzes Herz zerfleischt.
Der Rache Dunkel sei zerrissen,
Sieh' her! Du hast mich nicht getäuscht!
Pizarro, den du stürzen wolltest,
Pizarro, den du fürchten solltest,
Steht nun als Rächer hier.

Florestan:
Ein Mörder steht vor mir!

Pizarro:
Noch einmal ruf ich dir,
Was du getan, zurück;
Nur noch ein Augenblick
Und dieser Dolch...

Leonore:
Zurück!

Florestan:
O Gott!

Rocco:
Was soll?

Leonore:
Durchbohren musst du erst diese Brust;
Der Tod sei dir geschworen
Für deine Mörderlust.

Pizarro:
Wahnsinniger!

Rocco:
Halt ein!

Pizarro:
Er soll bestrafet sein!

Pizarro:
No, but unchain him from the stone.
Time is pressing.

Pizarro:
He shall die here!
But first he shall be told.
I'll tear his proud heart to pieces, and
then the dark veil of revenge will be torn.
Look here! You could not deceive me!
Pizarro, whom you hoped to bring to his
end, Pizarro, whom you ought to fear,
faces you as avenger.

Florestan:
A murderer faces me!

Pizarro:
You shall recall once again
what you have done to me;
Only one short moment
and this steel...

Leonore:
Stand back!

Florestan:
Oh God!

Rocco:
What's happening?

Leonore:
You must first pierce my heart;
I have sworn death to you
for your murderous lust.

Pizarro:
Madman!

Rocco:
Stop it!

Pizarro:
He shall be punished!

Leonore:
Töt' erst sein Weib!

Rocco, Pizarro:
Sein Weib?

Florestan:
Mein Weib?

Leonore:
Ja, sieh' hier Leonore!

Florestan:
Leonore!

Leonore:
Ich bin sein Weib, geschworen
Hab' ich ihm Trost. Verderben dir!

Pizarro:
Welch unerhörter Mut!

Florestan:
Vor Freude starrt mein Blut!

Rocco:
Mir starrt vor Angst mein Blut.

Leonore:
Ich trotze seiner Wut!

Pizarro:
Soll ich vor einem Weibe beben?

Leonore:
Der Tod sei dir geschworen.

Pizarro:
So opfr' ich beide meinem Grimm.

Leonore:
Durchbohren musst du erst diese Brust!

Pizarro:
Geteilt hast du mit ihm das Leben,
So teile nun den Tod mit ihm.

Leonore:
First kill his wife!

Rocco, Pizarro:
His wife?

Florestan:
My wife?

Leonore:
Yes, here you see Leonore!

Florestan:
Leonore!

Leonore:
I am his wife. I vowed to help him,
and vowed death to you!

Pizarro:
What unheard of courage!

Florestan:
My heart stops! I am overjoyed!

Rocco:
My heart stops out of fear.

Leonore:
I shall defy his wrath.

Pizarro:
Shall I fear a woman?

Leonore:
I have sworn death for you.

Pizarro:
Both of you shall be my hated victims.

Leonore:
You must pierce this heart first!

Pizarro:
You have shared your life with him;
you shall now share his death with him.

Leonore:
Noch einen Laut - und du bist tot!
Ach! Du bist gerettet! Grosser Gott!

Leonore:
One more word - and you'll be dead!
Ah! You are saved! Great God!

Florestan:
Ach! Ich bin gerettet! Grosser Gott!

Florestan:
Ah! I am saved! Great God!

Pizarro:
Ha! Der Minister! Höll' und Tod!

Pizarro:
Ah! The Minister! Hell and Death!

Rocco:
O was ist das! Gerechter Gott!

Rocco:
Oh! What is this! A Gracious God!

Jaquino:
Vater Rocco, Vater Rocco, der Herr
Minister kommt an, sein Gefolge ist
schon vor dem Schlosstor.

Jaquino:
Father Rocco, the Minister is arriving,
his retinue is already in front of the
castle-gates.

Rocco:
Gelobt sei Gott! Wir kommen, ja wir
kommen augenblicklich. Und unsere
Leute sollen heruntersteigen und den
Herrn Gouverneur hinaufbegleiten.

Rocco:
The Lord be praised! We are coming, yes,
we are coming, at once. And our men
shall come down to accompany the
governors.

Quartet: Leonore, Florestan:
Es schlägt der Rache Stunde.
Du (ich) soll(st) gerettet sein;
Die Liebe wird im Bunde
Mit Mute dich (mich) befrein.

Leonore, Florestan:
The hour of vengeance has come.
This means you shall be saved;
the union of our love gave you courage
and made you free.

Pizarro:
Verflucht sei diese Stunde!
Die Heuchler spotten mein;
Verzweiflung wird im Bunde
Mit meiner Rache sein.

Pizarro:
Damned this fateful hour!
The traitors laugh at me;
Despair will now be united
with my revenge.

Rocco:
O fürchterliche Stunde!
O Gott, was wartet mein?
Ich will nicht mehr im Bunde
Mit diesem Wütrich sein.

Rocco:
Oh hour full of horror!
Oh God, what awaits me?
I will no longer be united
with this villain.

Pizarro rushes off, making a sign for Rocco to follow him.
Rocco seizes the hands of both Leonore and Florestan,
and points to heaven as a sign of gratitude.

Florestan:
O meine Leonore!

Leonore:
Florestan!

Florestan:
Was hast du für mich gethan?

Leonore:
Nichts, nichts, mein Florestan!

Duet: Leonore, Florestan:
O namenlose Freude!
Mein Mann an meiner Brust!

Florestan:
O namenlose Freude!
And Leonorens Brust!

Beide:
Nach unnennbarem Leide
So übergrosse Lust!

Leonore:
Du wieder nun in meinen Armen1

Florestan:
O Gott, wie gross ist dein Erbarmen!

Beide:
Mein Weib, mein Weib, an meiner Brust!
Mein Mann, mein Mann, an meiner
Brust! O dank dir, Gott, für diese Lust!

Florestan:
Du bist's!

Leonore:
Ich bin's!

Florestan:
O himmlisches Entzücken! Leonore!

Leonore:
Florestan!

Florestan:
O my Leonore!

Leonora:
Florestan!

Florestan:
What have you done for me?

Leonora:
Nothing, my Florestan!

Oh what boundless happiness!
My husband in my arms!

Florestan:
Oh what boundless happiness!
Leonore in my arms!

Both:
After untold sorrows
such unbelievable joy!

Leonore:
I hold you in my arms again!

Florestan:
Oh God, how great your mercy is!

Both:
My wife, I hold her in my arms!
My husband I hold in my arms!
We thank you, Lord, for this great bliss!

Florestan:
You here!

Leonore:
I'm here!

Florestan:
Oh heavenly delight!

Leonore:
Florestan!

Beide:
O namenlose Freude!
Mein Weib, mein Weib, an meiner Brust!
Du wieder mein, an meiner Brust!
O dank dir, Gott, für diese Lust!

Both:
Oh what boundless happiness!
My wife, I hold her in my arms!
My husband I hold in my arms!
We thank you, Lord, for this great bliss!

*The Prisoners, Don Fernando, Pizarro, Marzelline and Jaquino,
plus the entire populace and guards surround the prisoners.
The Minister and his retinue enter through tthe castle gate.
The prisoners fall upon their knees.*

Alle:
Heil sei dem Tag, Heil sei der Stunde,
Die lang ersehnt, doch unvermeint,
Gerechtigkeit mit Huld im Bunde
Vor unsres Grabes Tor erscheint!

All:
Blessed the day, blessed the hour,
we longed for, but with little hope.
Justice has come with graciousness in
union to the gate of our graves!

Fernando:
Des besten Königs Wink und Wille
Führt mich zu euch, ihr Armen, her,
Dass ich der Frevel Nacht enthülle,
Die all' umfangen schwarz und schwer.
Nein, nicht länger knieet sklavisch nieder,
Tyrannenstrenge sei mir fern.
Es sucht der Bruder seine Brüder,
Und kann er helfen, hilft er gern.

Fernando:
Our gracious Majesty's will and pleasure
has sent me here to you unfortunate men,
that I disclose the crimes of darkness
which, has enveloped all of you. No
longer kneel like slaves before me.
I detest a tyrant's grimness.
A brother has come to seek his brethren,
and he can help, and gladly helps.

Rocco:
Wohlan, so helfet! Helft den Armen!

Rocco:
Well, Sir, you help now! Help the poor!

Pizarro:
Was seh' ich? Ha!

Pizarro:
What do I see?

Rocco:
Bewegt es dich?

Rocco:
Are you moved now?

Pizarro:
Fort! Fort!

Pizarro:
Away! Away!

Fernando:
Nun, rede!

Fernando:
No! Speak up!

Rocco:
All Erbarmen
Vereine diesem Paare
Don Florestan -

Rocco:
All your mercy
be given to this pair.
Don Florestan -

Fernando:
Der Totgeglaubte,
Der Edle, der für Wahrheit stritt?

Fernando:
The noble man who fought for truth
whom we thought dead?

Rocco:
Und Qualen ohne Zahl erlitt.

Rocco:
And suffered numberless tortures.

Fernando:
Mein Freund! Mein Freund!
Der Totgeglaubte? Gefesselt, bleich steht
er vor mir.

Fernando:
My friend! My friend!
He is alive?
He faces me pale, and in chains.

Rocco, Leonore:
Ja, Florestan, Ihr seht ihn hier.

Rocco, Leonore:
Yes, Florestan, you see him here.

Rocco:
Und Leonore -

Rocco:
And Leonore -

Fernando:
Leonore?

Fernando:
Leonore?

Rocco:
Der Frauen Zierde führ' ich vor.
Sie kam hierher -

Rocco:
The best of wives I bring here for you.
She came to me -

Pizarro:
Zwei Worte sagen -

Pizarro:
Two words allow me -

Fernando:
Kein Wort! Sie kam -

Fernando:
No more! She came -

Rocco:
Dort an mein Tor,
Und trat als Knecht in meine Dienste,
Und tat so brave, treue Dienste,
Dass ich - zum Eidam sie erkor.

Rocco:
There, to my door,
she became my servant,
and worked so loyally for me
that I made her my son-in-law.

Marzelline:
O weh' mir, was vernimmt mein Ohr!

Marzelline:
Dear me, what must I hear!

Rocco:
Der Unmensch wollt' in dieser Stunde
Vollziehn an Florestan den Mord.

Rocco:
This villain, in this very hour
he meant to murder Florestan.

Pizarro:
Vollziehn mit ihm!

Pizarro:
With his support!

Rocco:
Mit uns im Bunde!
Nur Euer Kommen rief ihn fort.

Rocco:
With your appearance, your arrival
enabled us to free him.

Alle:
Bestrafet sei der Bösewicht,
Der Unschuld unterdrückt.
Gerechtigkeit hält zum Gericht
Der Rache Schwert gezückt.

All:
Now let the villain be punished; the man
who oppressed the innocent.
Justice holds up the sword of vengeance
for all to witness.

Fernando:
Du schlossest auf des Edlen Grab,
Jetzt nimm ihm seine Ketten ab -
Doch halt! Euch, edle Frau, allein,
Euch ziemt es, ganz ihn zu befrein.

Fernando:
You unlocked this brave man's grave.
Now remove his chains!
But no! You, noble lady, you alone have
the honor to make him wholly free.

Quintet: Leonore:
O Gott! Welch ein Augenblick!

Leonore:
Oh Lord! What a glorious moment this is!

Florestan:
O unaussprechlich süsses Glück!

Florestan:
Oh what unspeakable happiness!

Fernando:
Gerecht, O Gott, ist dein Gericht.

Fernando:
Oh Lord, your judgment is just.

Marzelline, Rocco:
Du prüfest, du verlässt uns nicht.

Marzelline, Rocco:
You tempted us, you did not desert us.

Alle:
O Gott! O welch ein Augenblick !
O unaussprechlich süsses Glück!
Gerecht, O Gott, ist dein Gericht,
Du prüfest, du verlässt uns nicht!

All:
Oh Lord! What a moment this is!
Oh what unspeakable happiness!
O Lord, your judgment is just,
You tempt us, you did not desert us.

Wer ein holdes Weib errungen,
Stimm' in unsern Jubel ein!
Nie wird es zu hoch besungen,
Retterin des Gatten sein.

If you call a faithful wife one's own,
join in our song of joy!
You became your husband's savior.
Do not praise that too lightly.

Florestan:
Deine Treu' erhielt mein Leben,
Tugend schreckt den Bösewicht.

Florestan:
Your faithfulness has saved my life.
Virtue makes the villain fear.

Leonore:
Liebe führte mein Bestreben,
Wahre Liebe fürchtet nicht.

Leonore:
Love alone guides my efforts.
Real love has no fear.

Marzelline, Rocco:
Preist mit hoher Freude Glut
Leonorens edlen Mut.

Florestan:
Wer ein solches Weib
Stimm' in unsern Jubel ein!
Nie wird es zu hoch besungen,
Retterin des Gatten sein.

Leonore:
Liebend ist es mir gelungen,
Dich aus Ketten zu befrein.
Liebend sei es hoch besungen.
Florestan ist wieder mein!

Chor:
Wer ein holdes Weib errungen,
Stimm' in unsern Jubel ein!
Nie wird es zu hoch besungen,
Retterin des Gatten sein.

Leonore
Liebend sei es hoch besungen:
Florestan ist wieder mein!

Alle:
Nie wird es zu hoch besungen,
Retterin des Gatten sein!

Marzelline, Rocco:
Praise Leonora's noble mind with
greatest joy and warmth.
.

Florestan:
Whoever calls such a wife his own,
join in our song of joy!
Never praise too highly
the forthcoming rescue of a husband.

Leonore:
To liberate you from your chains.
I sing lovingly with joy:
that you became your husband's savior,
and Florestan is mine again!

Chorus:
Who calls a faithful wife his own,
Join in our song of joy!
It is praised on high,
that you are the spouse's savior.

Leonore:
Lovingly I sing with joy:
Florestan is mine again!

All:
Never praise too highly
that you became your husband's savior!

End of Opera

DICTIONARY OF OPERA AND MUSICAL TERMS

Accelerando - Play the music faster, but gradually.

Adagio - At a slow or gliding tempo, not as slow as largo, but not as fast as andante.

Agitato - Restless or agitated.

Allegro - At a brisk or lively tempo, faster than andante but not as fast as presto.

Andante - A moderately slow, easy-going tempo.

Appoggiatura - An extra or embellishing note preceding a main melodic note. Usually written as a note of smaller size, it shares the time value of the main note.

Arabesque - Flourishes or fancy patterns usually applying to vocal virtuosity.

Aria - A solo song usually structured in a formal pattern. Arias generally convey reflective and introspective thoughts rather than descriptive action.

Arietta - A shortened form of aria.

Arioso - A musical passage or composition having a mixture of free recitative and metrical song.

Arpeggio - Producing the tones of a chord in succession rather than simultaneously.

Atonal - Music that is not anchored in traditional musical tonality; it does not use the diatonic scale and has no keynote or tonal center.

Ballad opera - Eighteenth-century English opera consisting of spoken dialogue and music derived from popular ballad and folksong sources. The most famous is *The Beggar's Opera,* which is a satire of the Italian opera seria.

Bar - A vertical line across the stave that divides the music into measures.

Baritone - A male singing voice ranging between bass and tenor.

Baroque - A style of artistic expression prevalent in the 17th century that is marked by the use of complex forms, bold ornamentation, and florid decoration. The Baroque period extends from approximately 1600 to 1750 and includes the works of the original creators of modern opera, the Camerata, as well as the later works by Bach and Handel.

Bass - The lowest male voice, usually divided into categories such as:

Basso buffo - A bass voice that specializes in comic roles: Dr. Bartolo in Rossini's *The Barber of Seville.*

Basso cantante - A bass voice that demonstrates melodic singing quality: King Philip in Verdi's *Don Carlos.*

Basso profundo - the deepest, most profound, or most dramatic of bass voices: Sarastro in Mozart's *The Magic Flute.*

Bel canto - Literally, "beautiful singing." It originated in Italian opera of the 17th and 18th centuries and stressed beautiful tones produced with ease, clarity, purity, and evenness, together with an agile vocal technique and virtuosity. Bel canto flourished in the first half of the 19th century in the works of Rossini, Bellini, and Donizetti.

Cabaletta - A lively, concluding portion of an aria or duet. The term is derived from the Italian word "cavallo," or horse: it metaphorically describes a horse galloping to the finish line.

Cadenza - A flourish or brilliant part of an aria (or concerto) commonly inserted just before a finale. It is usually performed without accompaniment.

Camerata - A gathering of Florentine writers and musicians between 1590 and 1600 who attempted to recreate what they believed was the ancient Greek theatrical synthesis of drama, music, and stage spectacle; their experimentation led to the creation of the early structural forms of modern opera.

Cantabile - An indication that the singer should sing sweetly.

Cantata - A choral piece generally containing Scriptural narrative texts: the *St. Matthew Passion* of Bach.

Cantilena - Literally, "little song." A lyrical melody meant to be played or sung "cantabile," or with sweetness and expression.

Canzone - A short, lyrical operatic song usually containing no narrative association with the drama but rather simply reflecting the character's state of mind: Cherubino's "Voi che sapete" in Mozart's *The Marriage of Figaro.*

Castrato - A young male singer who was surgically castrated to retain his treble voice.

Cavatina - A short aria popular in 18th and 19th century opera that usually heralded the entrance of a principal singer.

Classical Period - A period roughly between the Baroque and Romantic periods, the late 18th through the early 19th centuries. Stylistically, the music of the period stresses clarity, precision, and rigid structural forms.

Coda - A trailer added on by the composer after the music's natural conclusion. The coda serves as a formal closing to the piece.

Coloratura - Literally, "colored": it refers to a soprano singing in the bel canto tradition. It is a singing technique that requires great agility, virtuosity, embellishments and ornamentation: The Queen of the Night's aria, "Zum Leiden bin ich auserkoren," from Mozart's *The Magic Flute*.

Commedia dell'arte - A popular form of dramatic presentation originating in Renaissance Italy in which highly stylized characters were involved in comic plots involving mistaken identities and misunderstandings. Two of the standard characters were Harlequin and Colombine: The "play within a play" in Leoncavallo's *I Pagliacci*.

Comprimario - A singer who performs secondary character roles such as confidantes, servants, and messengers.

Continuo, Basso continuo - A bass part (as for a keyboard or stringed instrument) that was used especially in baroque ensemble music; it consists of an independent succession of bass notes that indicate the required chords and their appropriate harmonies. Also called *figured bass, thoroughbass*.

Contralto - The lowest female voice, derived from "contra" against, and "alto" voice; a voice between the tenor and mezzo-soprano.

Countertenor - A high male voice generally singing within the female high soprano ranges.

Counterpoint - The combination of two or more independent melodies into a single harmonic texture in which each retains its linear character. The most sophisticated form of counterpoint is the fugue form, in which from two to six melodies can be used; the voices are combined, each providing a variation on the basic theme but each retaining its relation to the whole.

Crescendo - A gradual increase in the volume of a musical passage.

Da capo - Literally, "from the top"; repeat. Early 17th-century da capo arias were in the form of A B A, with the second A section repeating the first, but with ornamentation.

Deus ex machina - Literally "god out of a machine." A dramatic technique in which a person or thing appears or is introduced suddenly and unexpectedly; it provides a contrived solution to an apparently insoluble dramatic difficulty.

Diatonic - A major or minor musical scale that comprises intervals of five whole steps and two half steps.

Diminuendo - Gradually becoming softer; the opposite of crescendo.

Dissonance - A mingling of discordant sounds that do not harmonize within the diatonic scale.

Diva - Literally, "goddess"; generally the term refers to a leading female opera star who either possesses, or pretends to possess, great rank.

Dominant - The fifth tone of the diatonic scale; in the key of C, the dominant is G.

Dramatic soprano or tenor - A voice that is powerful, possesses endurance, and is generally projected in a declamatory style.

Dramma giocoso - Literally, "amusing (or humorous) drama." An opera whose story combines both serious and comic elements: Mozart's *Don Giovanni*.

Falsetto - A lighter or "false" voice; an artificially-produced high singing voice that extends above the range of the full voice.

Fioritura - It., "flowering"; a flowering ornamentation or embellishment of the vocal line within an aria.

Forte, fortissimo - Forte (*f*) means loud; mezzo forte (*mf*) is fairly loud; fortissimo (*ff*) is even louder; additional *fff*'s indicate greater degrees of loudness.

Glissando - Literally, "gliding." A rapid sliding up or down the scale.

Grand opera - An opera in which there is no spoken dialogue and the entire text is set to music, frequently treating serious and tragic subjects. Grand opera flourished in France in the 19th century (Meyerbeer); the genre is epic in scale and combines spectacle, large choruses, scenery, and huge orchestras.

Heldentenor - A tenor with a powerful dramatic voice who possesses brilliant top notes and vocal stamina. Heldentenors are well suited to heroic (Wagnerian) roles: Lauritz Melchior in Wagner's *Tristan und Isolde*.

Imbroglio - Literally, "intrigue"; an operatic scene portraying chaos and confusion, with appropriate diverse melodies and rhythms.

Largo or larghetto - Largo indicates a very slow tempo, broad and with dignity. Larghetto is at a slightly faster tempo than largo.

Legato - Literally, "tied" or "bound"; successive tones that are connected smoothly. The opposite of legato is staccato (short and plucked tones.)

Leitmotif - Literally, "leading motive." A musical fragment characterizing a person, thing, feeling, or idea that provides associations when it recurs.

Libretto - Literally, "little book"; the text of an opera.

Lied - A German song; the plural is "lieder." Originally, a German art song of the late 18th century.

Lyric - A voice that is light and delicate.

Maestro - From the Italian "master"; a term of respect to conductors, composers, directors, and great musicians.

Melodrama - Words spoken over music. Melodrama appears in Beethoven's *Fidelio* and flourished during the late 19th century in the operas of Massenet (*Manon* and *Werther*).

Mezza voce - Literally, "medium voice"; singing with medium or half volume. It is sometimes intended as a vocal means to intensify emotion.

Mezzo-soprano - A woman's voice with a range between soprano and contralto.

Obbligato - An accompaniment to a solo or principal melody that is usually played by an important, single instrument.

Octave - A musical interval embracing eight diatonic degrees; from C to C is an octave.

Opera - Literally, "work"; a dramatic or comic play in which music is the primary vehicle that conveys its story.

Opera buffa - Italian comic opera that flourished during the bel canto era. Highlighting the opera buffa genre were buffo characters who were usually basses singing patter songs: Dr. Bartolo in Rossini's *The Barber of Seville*; Dr. Dulcamara in Donizetti's *The Elixir of Love.*

Opéra comique - A French opera characterized by spoken dialogue interspersed between the musical numbers, as opposed to grand opera in which there is no spoken dialogue. Opéra comique subjects can be either comic or tragic.

Operetta, or light opera - Operas that contain comic elements and generally a light romantic plot: Strauss's *Die Fledermaus*, Offenbach's *La Périchole*, and Lehar's *The Merry Widow.* In operettas, there is usually much spoken dialogue, dancing, practical jokes, and mistaken identities.

Oratorio - A lengthy choral work, usually of a religious nature and consisting chiefly of recitatives, arias, and choruses, but performed without action or scenery: Handel's *Messiah.*

Ornamentation - Extra embellishing notes—appoggiaturas, trills, roulades, or cadenzas—that enhance a melodic line.

Overture - The orchestral introduction to a musical dramatic work that sometimes incorporates musical themes within the work. Overtures are instrumental pieces that are generally performed independently of their respective operas in concert.

Parlando - Literally, "speaking"; the imitation of speech while singing, or singing that is almost speaking over the music. Parlando sections are usually short and have minimal orchestral accompaniment.

Patter song - A song with words that are rapidly and quickly delivered. Figaro's "Largo al factotum" in Rossini's *The Barber of Seville* is a patter song.

Pentatonic - A five-note scale. Pentatonic music is most prevalent in Far Eastern countries.

Piano - A performance indication for soft volume.

Pitch - The property of a musical tone that is determined by the frequency of the waves producing it.

Pizzicato - An indication that notes are to be played by plucking the strings instead of stroking the string with the bow.

Polyphony - Literally, "many voices." A style of musical composition in which two or more independent melodies are juxtaposed; counterpoint.

Polytonal - Several tonal schemes used simultaneously.

Portamento - A continuous gliding movement from one tone to another through all the intervening pitches.

Prelude - An orchestral introduction to an act or a whole opera that precedes the opening scene.

Presto, prestissimo - Vigorous, and with the utmost speed.

Prima donna - Literally, "first lady." The female star or principal singer in an opera cast or opera company.

Prologue - A piece sung before the curtain goes up on the opera proper: Tonio's Prologue in Leoncavallo's *I Pagliacci.*

Quaver - An eighth note.

Range - The span of tonal pitch of a particular voice: soprano, mezzo-soprano, contralto, tenor, baritone, and bass.

Recitative - A formal device used to advance the plot. It is usually sung in a rhythmically free vocal style that imitates the natural inflections of speech; it conveys the dialogue and narrative in operas and oratorios. *Secco*, or dry, recitative is accompanied by harpsichord and sometimes with other continuo instruments; *accompagnato* indicates that the recitative is accompanied by the orchestra.

Ritornello - A refrain, or short recurrent instrumental passage between elements of a vocal composition.

Romanza - A solo song that is usually sentimental; it is shorter and less complex than an aria and rarely deals with terror, rage, or anger.

Romantic Period - The Romantic period is usually considered to be between the early 19th and early 20th centuries. Romanticists found inspiration in nature and man. Von Weber's *Der Freischütz* and Beethoven's *Fidelio* (1805) are considered the first German Romantic operas; many of Verdi's operas as well as the early operas of Wagner are also considered Romantic operas.

Roulade - A florid, embellished melody sung to one syllable.

Rubato - An expressive technique, literally meaning "robbed"; it is a fluctuation of tempo within a musical phrase, often against a rhythmically steady accompaniment.

Secco - "Dry"; the type of accompaniment for recitative played by the harpsichord and sometimes continuo instruments.

Semitone - A half step, the smallest distance between two notes. In the key of C, the half steps are from E to F and from B to C.

Serial music - Music based on a series of tones in a chosen pattern without regard for traditional tonality.

Sforzando - Sudden loudness and force; it must stand out from the texture and be emphasized by an accent.

Singspiel - Literally, "song drama." Early German style of opera employing spoken dialogue between songs: Mozart's *The Magic Flute.*

Soprano - The highest range of the female voice ranging from lyric (light and graceful quality) to dramatic (fuller and heavier in tone).

Sotto voce - Literally, "below the voice"; sung softly between a whisper and a quiet conversational tone.

Soubrette - A soprano who sings supporting roles in comic opera: Adele in Strauss's *Die Fledermaus*; Despina in Mozart's *Così fan tutte.*

Spinto - From the Italian "spingere" (to push); a singer with lyric vocal qualities who "pushes" the voice to achieve heavier dramatic qualities.

Sprechstimme - Literally, "speaking voice." The singer half sings a note and half speaks; the declamation sounds like speaking but the duration of pitch makes it seem almost like singing.

Staccato - Short, clipped, detached, rapid articulation; the opposite of legato.

Stretto - Literally, "narrow." A concluding passage performed in a quick tempo to create a musical climax.

Strophe - Strophe is a rhythmic system of repeating lines. A musical setting of a strophic text is characterized by the repetition of the same music for all strophes.

Syncopation - A shifting of the beat forward or back from its usual place in the bar; a temporary displacement of the regular metrical accent in music caused typically by stressing the weak beat.

Supernumerary - A "super"; a performer with a non-singing and non-speaking role: "Spear-carrier."

Symphonic poem - A large orchestral work in one continuous movement, usually narrative or descriptive in character: Franz Liszt's *Les Preludes*; Richard Strauss's *Don Juan, Till Eulenspiegel,* and *Ein Heldenleben.*

Tempo - The speed at which music is performed.

Tenor - The highest natural male voice.

Tessitura - The usual range of a voice part.

Tonality - The organization of all the tones and harmonies of a piece of music in relation to a tonic (the first tone of its scale).

Tone poem - An orchestral piece with a program.

Tonic - The principal tone of the key in which a piece is written. C is the tonic of C major.

Trill - Two adjacent notes rapidly and repeatedly alternated.

Tutti - All together.

Twelve-tone - The twelve chromatic tones of the octave placed in a chosen fixed order and constituting, with some permitted permutations and derivations, the melodic and harmonic material of a serial musical piece. Each note of the chromatic scale is used as part of the melody before any other note is repeated.

Verismo - Literally "truth"; the artistic use of contemporary everyday material in preference to the heroic or legendary in opera. A movement particularly in Italian opera during the late 19th and early 20th centuries: Mascagni's *Cavalleria rusticana*.

Vibrato - A "vibration"; a slightly tremulous effect imparted to vocal or instrumental tone to enrich and intensify sound, and add warmth and expressiveness through slight and rapid variations in pitch.

Opera Journeys™ Mini Guide Series

Opera Journeys™ Libretto Series

Opera Classics Library™ Series

A History of Opera: Milestones and Metamorphoses

Puccini Companion: the Glorious Dozen

Mozart's da Ponte Operas

Fifty Timeless Opera Classics

PUCCINI COMPANION: THE GLORIOUS DOZEN

756-page Soft Cover volume

Each Puccini Chapter features:

COMPLETE LIBRETTO
Italian-English side-by-side

STORY NARRATIVE
with 100s of Music Highlight Examples

ANALYSIS AND COMMENTARY

Print or Ebook

A HISTORY of OPERA: MILESTONES and METAMORPHOSES

432 pages, soft cover / 21 chapters
featuring **Over 250 music examples**

• A comprehensive survey of milestones in opera history
• All periods are analyzed in depth:
Baroque, Classical, Romantic, Bel Canto, Opera Buffa, German Romanticism, Wagner and music drama, Verismo,
plus analyses of the "Tristan Chord," atonalism, minimalism...

Print or Ebook

OPERA JOURNEYS' COLLECTION: FIFTY TIMELESS OPERA CLASSICS

816-page Soft Cover volume

Print or EBook

*A collection of fifty·of the most popular operas
in the Opera Journeys Mini Guide Series,
each with Story Narrative and 100s of Music Examples,
PLUS insightful,in delpth commentary and analysis*

MOZART'S DA PONTE OPERAS:

Don Giovanni, The Marriage of Figaro, Così fan tutte

348-page Soft or Hard Cover Edition

Print or Ebook

Mozart: Master of Musical Characterization;
Da Ponte: Ambassador of Italian Culture.

*Featuring: Principal Characters, Brief Story Synopsis, Story Narrative, Music 'Highlight Examples, and insightful in depth Commentary and Analysis, PLUS
a newly translated LIBRETTO of each opera
with Italian/English translation side-by-side.*

ORDER: Opera Journeys' Web Site www.operajourneys.com

OPERA JOURNEYS LIBRETTO SERIES

Print or Ebook

New translations (side-by-side) with Music Highlight Examples

•Aida •The Barber of Seville •La Bohème
•Carmen •Cavalleria Rusticana •La Cenerentola
•Così fan tutte •Don Carlo •Don Giovanni
•La Fanciulla del West •Gianni Schicchi
•Lucia di Lammermoor •Madama Butterfly
•The Magic Flute •Manon Lescaut
•The Marriage of Figaro •A Masked Ball
•Otello •I Pagliacci •Rigoletto •La Rondine
•Salome Samson and Delilah •Suor Angelica
•Il Tabarro •Tosca •La Traviata •Il Trovatore •Turandot

OPERA JOURNEYS MINI GUIDE SERIES

Print or Ebook

featuring 125 titles

• *Brief Story Synopsis*

• *Principal Characters*

• *Story Narrative*

• *Music Highlight Examples*

• *Commentary and Analysis*

•The Abduction from the Seraglio •Adriana Lecouvreur •L'Africaine •Aida •Andrea Chénier
•Anna Bolena •Ariadne auf Naxos •Armida •Attila •The Ballad of Baby Doe •The Barber of Seville
•Duke Bluebeard's Castle •La Bohème •Boris Godunov •Candide •Capriccio •Carmen
•Cavalleria Rusticana •Cendrillon •La Cenerentola •La Clemenza di Tito •Le Comte Ory
•Così fan tutte •The Crucible •La Damnation de Faust •The Death of Klinghoffer •Doctor Atomic
• Don Carlo • Don Giovanni •Don Pasquale •La Donna del Lago •The Elixir of Love •Elektra •Ernani
•Eugene Onegin •Falstaff •La Fanciulla del West •Faust •La Fille du Régiment
•Fidelio •Die Fledermaus •The Flying Dutchman •Die Frau ohne Schatten
•Der Freischütz •Gianni Schicchi •La Gioconda •Hamlet •Hansel and Gretel •Henry VIII
•Iolanta •L'Italiana in Algeri •Les Huguenots •Iphigénie en Tauride •Julius Caesar •Lakmé
•Lohengrin •Lucia di Lammermoor •Macbeth •Madama Butterfly •The Magic Flute
•The Makropolis Case •Manon •Manon Lescaut •Maria Stuarda •The Marriage of Figaro
•A Masked Ball •Die Meistersinger •The Mikado •Nabucco •Nixon in China •Norma
•Of Mice and Men •Orfeo ed Euridice •Otello •I Pagliacci •Parsifal •The Pearl Fishers
•Pelléas et Mélisande •Porgy and Bess •Prince Igor •I Puritani •The Queen of Spades
•The Rake's Progress •The Rape of Lucretia •The Rhinegold •Rigoletto •The Ring of the Nibelung
•Roberto Devereaux •Rodalinda •Roméo et Juliette •La Rondine •Der Rosenkavalier •Rusalka
•Salome •Samson and Delilah •Show Boat •Siegfried •Simon Boccanegra •La Sonnambula
•Suor Angelica •Susannah •Il Tabarro •The Tales of Hoffmann •Tannhäuser •Thaïs •Tosca
•La Traviata •Tristan and Isolde •Il Trittico •Les Troyens •Il Trovatore •Turandot
•Twilight of the Gods •The Valkyrie •Werther •West Side Story •Wozzeck

ORDER: Opera Journeys' Web Site www.operajourneys.com

Made in the USA
Middletown, DE
08 December 2019

80227331R00060